REGULATION AND ECONOMIC GROWTH

Regulation and Economic Growth

Applying Economic Theory to Public Policy

JAMES BROUGHEL

MERCATUS CENTER
George Mason University

Arlington, Virginia

ABOUT THE MERCATUS CENTER AT GEORGE MASON UNIVERSITY

The Mercatus Center at George Mason University is the world's premier university source for market-oriented ideas—bridging the gap between academic ideas and real-world problems.

A university-based research center, Mercatus advances knowledge about how markets work to improve people's lives by training graduate students, conducting research, and applying economics to offer solutions to society's most pressing problems.

Our mission is to generate knowledge and understanding of the institutions that affect the freedom to prosper and to find sustainable solutions that overcome the barriers preventing individuals from living free, prosperous, and peaceful lives.

Founded in 1980, the Mercatus Center is located on George Mason University's Arlington and Fairfax campuses.

Mercatus Center at George Mason University
3434 Washington Blvd., 4th Floor
Arlington, VA 22201
www.mercatus.org
703-993-4930

978-1-942951-36-0 paperback
978-1-942951-37-7 kindle ebook

Cover design by Amanda Weiss
Composition by Westchester Publishing Services, Danbury, CT
Editorial services by Publications Professionals

For Anna and Ellie

CONTENTS

FOREWORD

I f we consider the economy of the United States from the end of the Civil War to the present, a unique story of sustained, exponential growth emerges. Over those nearly 150 years, GDP per person in the United States grew by an average of about 2 percent annually, increasing nearly 17-fold.[1] In fact, that average growth rate looks even more remarkable if we start in 1930 (thus including the years of the Great Depression) and move forward to the present. Over those 85 years, the economy grew by 3.4 percent per year on average.

Yet these are not the stories we hear about economic growth today. Instead, recent growth trends have led to the resurgence of terms such as *secular stagnation* and the *new normal*, both of which hint at acceptance of slower growth going forward. Indeed, annual growth from 1970 to today has averaged only 2.8 percent, and it has been 10 years since growth of 3 percent or more was last observed. Total factor productivity growth has declined even more precipitously since the halcyon years of the mid-20th century. The start-up rate has followed a decades-long downward trend, while larger and older firms tend to persist longer than they used to—painting a picture of declining economic dynamism.

Debates continue over the causes of what some have called the end of US economic growth. In a recent piece titled "Doomed to Stagnate?," *Wall Street Journal* columnist Bret Stephens describes the case for stagnation as a "macro" argument caused by demographics (an aging population means a shrinking workforce), too much saving and too little investment, and inadequate innovation to make up the difference with productivity gains.[2] In contrast, writes Stephens, a "micro" argument might explain the broad and negative trends by referring to specific institutions that have arisen over recent decades to impede investment and growth, with regulation playing the role of prime suspect.

This book offers a road map for economists who would delve deeper into the causes of slower growth and declining dynamism. Economists, like their peers in many hard sciences, build quantitative models that permit the testing of competing theories with empirical data. James Broughel explains how regulation could be considered in economic growth models, ranging from neoclassical growth models such as the Solow model to the more recent endogenous growth models of Paul Romer and other researchers. Along the way, Broughel offers insights into the numerous models covered, pointing out their key features, their strengths, and their shortcomings.

Although Broughel thoroughly documents the significant progress of economic growth models, he also points out that many puzzles remain, including how to treat informal institutions such as social and cultural norms. Nonetheless, this wide-ranging book offers more than a foundation for researchers interested in how regulation affects growth. Broughel distills numerous lessons about regulation and growth that remain true regardless of the unsolved puzzles. Perhaps the most salient is that growth depends heavily on innovation, and the cumulative effect of regulations built up for decades can create a substantial barrier to innovation.

Until recently, most economists have not examined regulation—and more specifically, regulatory accumulation—as a determinant of economic growth. Perhaps this lack of examination can be explained by a lack of data, or perhaps it is because expertise in regulation and the regulatory process is often considered the domain of legal scholars instead of economists. Whatever the cause, the effect is similar to the proverbial search for car keys under a streetlight. If regulation is a major cause of slower growth, then a search for answers using models that fail to consider regulation's role will continue to be fruitless. Broughel's book, along with recent innovations in quantifying regulation to produce tractable data for use in growth models, has effectively built a new streetlight.

—Patrick A. McLaughlin
Program for Economic Research on Regulation
Mercatus Center at George Mason University

Introduction

This book presents a framework for assessing the economic growth implications of public policies, with particular attention given to the effects of government regulations on growth. The framework is intended to be a theoretical contribution to the field of regulatory economics, surveying the landscape of economic growth models and highlighting lessons from the models for regulatory policy. With a stronger theoretical foundation in place, regulators may be able to gain new insights into how regulations affect national income and, by extension, other important indicators of human well-being.

When economists talk about *economic growth,* they are referring to changes in national income. Typically, such changes are evaluated using measures of a country's GDP, defined as the market value of final goods and services produced inside a country's borders in a single year. GDP is a measure of the value of a nation's annual output and also of its income. Economic growth is typically measured in changes in *real* GDP, where *real* reflects that adjustments are made to account for a changing price level over time.

GDP per capita (meaning GDP divided by the population of the country) is a reasonable approximation of a nation's standard of living, just as personal income is a reasonable measure of an individual's standard of living.

GDP per capita is correlated with many important indicators of well-being, such as life expectancy, and negatively correlated with characteristics that countries want to avoid, such as child mortality and corruption. There are some well-known limitations to using GDP as a measure of living standards. For example, GDP misses activity not traded in markets, such as unpaid housework and the value that people derive from leisure time. However, as a measure of a nation's annual income, GDP is reasonably accurate. Income is not an all-encompassing measure of human well-being, of course, but income is used to purchase the goods and services that matter most to people's health, happiness, and quality of life. Therefore, income is an important measure of well-being, even if other measures of well-being are also important.

Regulations—the other focus of this book—are restrictions on human behavior. Restrictions may not always be legal in nature. For example, professional baseball teams follow regulations that govern how their game is played. These rules are set by the Major League Baseball organization. Here, the focus is on legal regulations that are promulgated by government agencies. Regulations, as written by administrative agencies, are distinguished from laws written by legislatures, which consist of elected representatives of the people. Administrative agencies employ public officials who, more often than not, are career public servants. These officials are delegated law-making authority from legislatures. Furthermore, regulations are unique in that—unlike taxes and spending—the vast majority of their effects are not captured in government budgets. In this sense, the effects of regulation are largely invisible to the public.

Although the focus of this book is on the effects of regulation on economic growth, there is little reason to think that regulations written by regulatory bodies are fundamentally different from laws written by legislatures or from other public policies. Therefore, this book should be useful to regulators and to students interested in the economic effects of regulation, but also to anyone interested in the growth implications of public policies in general.

The Fundamentals
of Economic Growth

Perhaps the most powerful lesson from economic growth theory is that small changes in output today can lead to enormous changes in living standards when those changes compound over time. This result led Nobel laureate Robert Lucas (1988, 5) to comment that "the consequences for human welfare involved in questions like these are simply staggering: Once one starts to think about [growth], it is hard to think about anything else."

The choices society makes today, for better or worse, can have huge implications for the welfare of future generations. If a society cares about the well-being of future generations, by extension, that society must care about economic growth. Seemingly minor mistakes or successes in public policy can have ripple effects that compound over time and change the course of history. As a result, those who set economic policy, such as elected officials and regulators, have a duty to be informed about the responsibility that comes with their power.

As will be shown in this book, not all causes of economic growth are known to economists. For example, some nontrivial component of growth appears to be an unintended consequence of human social interaction. Even today, many contributors to economic growth are debated or remain a mystery. This ambiguousness may leave some students of economic growth frustrated, and it means that to some extent policymakers must act under a great amount of uncertainty. But such is the current situation.

All is not lost, however. Economists do know enough to provide some fairly strong general guidelines for policymakers. The guidelines can assist regulators who seek to boost or—perhaps more important—avoid stifling economic growth. Those who write policy should keep these guidelines in mind as they balance the political demands of the moment with the long-term interests of the nation and future generations.

To understand the power of growth rate changes, table 2.1 presents hypothetical growth paths for an economy. Beginning in year 0—the present—this imaginary economy has a level of income per capita of $100. After just five years, a country whose per capita income is growing by 3 percent per year will enjoy a standard of living 10 percent higher than one that begins at the same level of income per capita but grows at just 1 percent. After 25 years, living standards are more than 60 percent higher in the country whose economy grows by 3 percent annually. And after 50 years, living standards are more than two and a half times higher than the economy that grows by 1 percent.

When the growth rate rises to 7 or 10 percent, these changes become even more astounding. A country whose economy grows by 7 percent per year in per capita terms will double incomes in just over a decade. A comparable change takes about 25 years when growing by 3 percent annually, and it takes almost 75 years when growing by 1 percent annually. Extending these rates far into the future, one can easily see that the implications for future

Table 2.1. Compounding at Different Growth Rates

Year	Growth rates			
	1%	3%	7%	10%
0	$100	$100	$100	$100
1	$101	$103	$107	$110
5	$105	$116	$140	$161
10	$110	$134	$197	$259
25	$128	$209	$543	$1,083
50	$164	$438	$2,946	$11,739
75	$211	$918	$15,988	$127,190
100	$270	$1,922	$86,772	$1,378,061

Source: Author's calculations.

generations are enormous. Speeding up the annual rate of economic growth by a single percentage point or two can change future living standards by orders of magnitude.

Table 2.1 presents a hypothetical example, of course; but now consider what has happened in the real world in recent decades. Table 2.2 presents growth rates for 55 countries for the years 1950–2014 (Feenstra, Inklaar, and Timmer 2015). Levels of GDP per capita at the beginning and end of the series are presented at purchasing power parity, as are compound annual per capita growth rates over this period. In comparing income and growth rates across countries, it is critical to make comparisons at purchasing power parity. Because countries typically evaluate their GDP using domestic currency, all GDPs must first be converted to a common metric, such as 2011 US dollars. Next, because one dollar may buy more in some countries (e.g., India) than others (e.g., Switzerland), adjustments must be made for the different price levels across countries.

Table 2.2. Changes in Income per Capita for a Sample of Countries, 1950–2014

Country	Real GDP per capita 1950 (2011 US$ PPP)	Real GDP per capita 2014 (2011 US$ PPP)	Compound annual growth rate (%)
Egypt	604	9,909	4.5
Japan	2,616	35,358	4.2
Thailand	1,072	13,967	4.1
El Salvador	673	7,843	3.9
Portugal	2,727	28,476	3.7
Cyprus	2,784	28,602	3.7
Germany	4,714	45,961	3.6
Spain	3,521	33,864	3.6
Ireland	5,126	48,767	3.6
Panama	2,152	19,702	3.5
Austria	5,340	47,744	3.5
Brazil	1,673	14,871	3.5
Italy	4,335	35,807	3.4
Luxembourg	12,083	95,176	3.3
Trinidad and Tobago	4,111	31,196	3.2
Norway	8,890	64,274	3.1
Argentina	2,890	20,222	3.1
Finland	5,961	40,401	3.0
Turkey	3,054	19,236	2.9
India	842	5,224	2.9
Netherlands	7,634	47,240	2.9
France	7,057	39,374	2.7
Morocco	1,312	7,163	2.7
Belgium	8,087	43,668	2.7
Peru	2,057	10,993	2.7
Ecuador	2,052	10,968	2.7

(continued)

Table 2.2. (*continued*)

Country	Real GDP per capita 1950 (2011 US$ PPP)	Real GDP per capita 2014 (2011 US$ PPP)	Compound annual growth rate (%)
Israel	6,267	33,270	2.6
Iceland	8,354	42,876	2.6
Denmark	9,473	44,924	2.5
Philippines	1,424	6,659	2.4
Sweden	10,002	44,598	2.4
Costa Rica	3,223	14,186	2.3
United Kingdom	9,263	40,242	2.3
Switzerland	13,960	58,469	2.3
Colombia	3,179	12,599	2.2
Ethiopia	336	1,323	2.2
Mauritius	4,665	17,942	2.1
Canada	11,248	42,352	2.1
Sri Lanka	2,765	10,342	2.1
Bolivia	1,661	6,013	2.0
Mexico	4,422	15,853	2.0
United States	14,655	52,292	2.0
Pakistan	1,333	4,646	2.0
Uruguay	6,259	20,396	1.9
Australia	13,310	43,071	1.9
Guatemala	2,374	6,851	1.7
New Zealand	12,402	34,735	1.6
Venezuela	5,862	14,134	1.4
South Africa	5,337	12,128	1.3
Uganda	854	1,839	1.2
Nigeria	2,623	5,501	1.2
Honduras	2,207	4,424	1.1
Kenya	1,590	2,769	0.9

(*continued*)

Table 2.2. (*continued*)

Country	Real GDP per capita 1950 (2011 US$ PPP)	Real GDP per capita 2014 (2011 US$ PPP)	Compound annual growth rate (%)
Nicaragua	3,404	4,453	0.4
Democratic Republic of the Congo	1,839	1,217	−0.6

Note: PPP = purchasing power parity.

Source: Author's calculations based on Feenstra, Inklaar, and Timmer 2015.

The fastest-growing countries in the group of 55 were Egypt and Japan, which grew at annualized rates of 4.5 and 4.2 percent, respectively. For Japan, this growth is quite impressive given that the country has experienced fairly slow growth in the past few decades and is a testament to how fast Japan grew early in the sample period. Rapid growth in Japan led per capita income to increase more than 10-fold, from just over $2,600 in 1950 to more than $35,000 in 2014 (2011 US$). Such a result is amazing in its own right, but it becomes even more impressive when contrasted with countries that were not nearly so fortunate. For example, in the Democratic Republic of the Congo, income per capita shrank during this period and left residents worse off by this measure in 2014 than their grandparents had been over 60 years earlier. The statistics do not fully account for some technological advancements, so these numbers likely underestimate improvements in living standards. Nonetheless, the stakes involved surrounding issues of economic growth are clear.

Some countries in table 2.2 grew faster in the latter half of the 20th century in part because they had to rebuild following World War II. Many European countries fall into this category. As will be seen in the review of the Solow model, a country can grow fast simply by destroying its capital stock. Such growth is not a good strategy for improving people's well-being, however, because it means initially lowering the *level* of income per capita. Both the level and the rate of growth of incomes are important for living standards.

Figure 2.1 shows the distribution of per capita growth rates across the countries listed in table 2.2. For the years 1950–2014, most countries experienced 1.0–3.9 percent growth per year. The United States grew at about 2 percent per annum during these years.

A natural question to ask when looking at figure 2.1 is the following: Given that economic growth in the range of 3–4 percent per year is clearly possible, what

Figure 2.1. Compound Annual Growth Rates in Real GDP per Capita for 55 Countries, 1950–2014

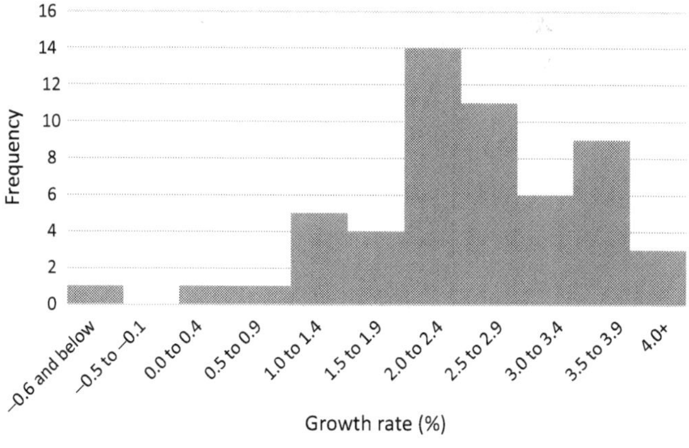

Source: Feenstra, Inklaar, and Timmer 2015.

can policymakers do to help achieve and maintain such a rate? A central purpose of this book is to shed light on this important question, with a particular emphasis on the role that regulatory policy can play as a promoter or an inhibitor of economic growth.

In the section that follows, this book examines one of the most widely used growth models in economics: the Solow model. This model should look familiar to most students who have taken an undergraduate macroeconomics course; it is a workhorse of modern macroeconomics. The next chapter presents a classification scheme to better understand the different outcomes that are possible following shocks to variables in the Solow model. With a classification scheme in place, newer growth models are reviewed, highlighting how regulation can affect the key variables in each model and, by extension, affect the growth path of the economy. Some of the remaining unsolved puzzles in growth theory, specifically those related to the roles of institutions and population as contributors to growth, will also be discussed. Armed with this framework, regulators should be better able to achieve their goals while keeping this nation's economy on a healthy, sustainable growth path.

THE SOLOW MODEL

To understand how individual regulations or groups of regulations affect economic growth, a model of economic growth is first needed. Models are necessary to make sense out of the complexity of the real world. Models simplify the world, thereby allowing better understanding of the forces that shape reality. The logical model to start our analysis with is the most famous of all growth models:

the Solow model. The model was developed by American economist Robert Solow (1956) and Australian economist Trevor Swan (1956) in the mid-20th century. This book uses a technology-augmented variant of the model, similar to versions in Charles I. Jones (2001) and David Romer (2011). "Technology augmented" means that technology is an input in the production process that works by increasing, or augmenting, the productivity of labor.

Throughout this book, variations are used of the famous Cobb–Douglas production function. That production follows a Cobb–Douglas form is a common assumption in many economic growth models. The function, developed by mathematicians Charles Cobb and Paul Douglas (1928), takes a form such as $Y = K^\alpha L^{1-\alpha}$, where Y represents the total output of the production process, and K and L represent capital and labor, respectively, which are the main inputs into the production process. The parameter α is the output elasticity of capital. It explains how output changes as the amount of capital used in production changes. Under conditions of perfect competition, α also represents the fraction of total output that is paid to capital.

Cobb–Douglas production functions are widely used in part because they capture very important real-world phenomena. For example, when $0 < \alpha < 1$, there are diminishing returns to capital and labor. This characteristic means that, as an economy adds more capital or labor to the production process, the additional output generated from each additional unit of input diminishes. This assumption is widely believed to be a realistic portrayal of actual production processes. For example, the first tractor put to work on a farm probably increases daily output by a substantial amount, but the fourth, fifth, or sixth tractor might not be of much use at all. This example highlights the phenomenon of diminishing marginal returns.

By allowing the exponents on capital and labor to sum to 1, the production function exhibits constant returns to all factors of production even while there are diminishing returns to individual factors. In other words, if the level of capital alone is doubled, output less than doubles (i.e., diminishing returns to capital), but if all inputs together are doubled (in this case, both capital and labor), output exactly doubles. Another convenient property of Cobb–Douglas production functions is that the elasticity of substitution between capital and labor is exactly 1, which means that a rise in the relative price of capital or labor will result in an equivalent decline in relative spending (in percentage terms) as firms substitute capital for labor and vice versa.

All these assumptions can be relaxed, of course, and changes in assumptions about the production process will have important implications for how government regulation changes output in any given model. To begin, however, let's keep things simple, assuming that production is explained by the equation

$$Y_t = f(K, AL) = K_t^\alpha (A_t L_t)^{1-\alpha}, 0 < \alpha < 1 \qquad (2.1)$$

where Y is the economy's total output, K is the amount of physical capital in the economy, A is an index of labor-augmenting technology, and L is the number of people employed in the labor force. The parameter α is capital's share of output, given the assumption of perfect competition. Because both α and $1 - \alpha$ are less than 1 but together sum to 1, this model exhibits diminishing returns to scale in the input factors $K, A,$ and $L,$ and constant returns to scale in all factors of production.

The levels of A and L at any given time t are explained by the equations

$$A_t = A_0 e^{gt} \qquad (2.2)$$

and

$$L_t = L_0 e^{nt}, \qquad (2.3)$$

such that A and L grow at the constant rates g and n, respectively, and begin from the levels A_0 and L_0.

It turns out that economic growth can be defined in two ways: *intensive form* (i.e., changes in output per unit of some input, such as labor) and *extensive form* (changes in total output). Quarterly releases of US GDP by the US Bureau of Economic Analysis relate to extensive growth. These are the numbers that regularly appear in newspapers. Economists typically work with the Solow model in intensive form, however, meaning variables are evaluated per unit of production input. Typically, the production input is labor, so variables of interest are divided by the number of workers in the economy. For example,

$$k_t = \frac{K_t}{A_t L_t} \qquad (2.4)$$

is the equation for capital in intensive form. Changes in per capita national income, such as those presented earlier in this chapter, are also measures of intensive growth. Here, however, k is the level of capital per *effective worker*, meaning capital per unit of technology-augmented labor. A key reason to care about effective workers is that workers' pay is based on their total productivity. In the real world, it is difficult to separate the productivity of an individual worker from the productivity of the technology that makes the worker more effective. For example, a firm cannot tell how much a worker contributes to its profit margins versus the electricity the worker uses at his or her desk, the car that transports him or her to work, or the computer he or she uses to write reports. It is assumed that workers capture benefits of technology in their wages. This assumption is reasonable because wage growth has tended to track productivity growth very closely over time.

A key element of the Solow model is the *capital accumulation equation*, which describes how the stock of capital per effective worker evolves over time:

$$\dot{k}_t = sy_t - (n + g + \delta)k_t. \tag{2.5}$$

Here, s is the fraction of national income that is saved, and δ represents the depreciation rate of capital. It is assumed that all savings in society are automatically invested in new capital. The variables n, s, g, and δ are *exogenous variables* in the model, which means these variables are determined outside the model itself and are simply given from the outset. Economists use models to predict *endogenous variables*—that is, variables that are explained in the system itself. In the Solow model, the most important endogenous variable is probably output per worker.

The variable $\dot{k}$ is the derivative of capital per effective worker with respect to time. In other words, it explains how much the capital stock changes at each point in time t. Equation (2.5) indicates that the change in the stock of capital per effective worker at time t is equal to what is added to the capital stock from investment (i.e., the fraction of income that is saved) minus what is needed to maintain *break-even investment* (i.e., the investment required to maintain a constant level of capital per effective worker).

To break even, investment at time t must add enough new k to account for labor force growth, technology growth, and depreciation.

An economy is at its *steady state* level of capital accumulation when $\dot{k} = 0$. At this point, capital per *effective* worker is constant, and it is fairly easy to show that output per *actual* worker solves to

$$\frac{Y_t}{L_t} = A_t \left(\frac{s}{n+g+\delta} \right)^{\frac{\alpha}{1-\alpha}} \tag{2.6}$$

in the steady state. Although capital per effective worker is constant in the steady state, capital per actual worker is not. It grows at rate g in the steady state, because all variables on the right-hand side of equation (2.6) are constant except for A, which is growing at rate g by assumption.

Equation (2.6) is also an equation for the *balanced growth path* of output per worker. An economy is operating along a balanced growth path when all variables in the model are growing at constant rates. A balanced growth path is achieved in the Solow model when the economy is at its steady state, with all per-*effective*-worker variables growing at the rate of 0; all per-*actual*-worker variables growing at rate g, as shown for Y/L in equation (2.6); and the aggregates K and Y growing at rate $n+g$.

A central finding of the Solow model is as follows: *The growth rate of output per worker along a balanced growth path is determined by the growth rate of technology.* This finding is not to say that other variables in the model, such as the savings rate or the labor force growth rate, are not important. Rather, permanent changes in these other variables influence the *level* of output per worker along a balanced growth path. Remember that levels and growth rates are both important. These other variables also influence growth rates as part of *transition dynamics*—that is, times when an economy is not operating along a balanced growth path. It turns out that economies are usually in the transition phase, not operating along a balanced growth path but instead moving toward one.

During transition periods, output per worker can grow faster than the technological growth rate g because the capital stock is growing. Capital per effective worker will accelerate or decelerate more quickly the further the economy is from the steady state. To calculate how fast the capital stock is growing, each side of the capital accumulation equation (2.5) is divided by k. This gives the instantaneous growth rate, $\dot{k}/k$, on the left-hand side of the equation. Figure 2.2 illustrates the growth rate dynamics of k and shows that the further the economy is from the steady

Figure 2.2. Acceleration and Deceleration of Growth in Capital per Effective Worker

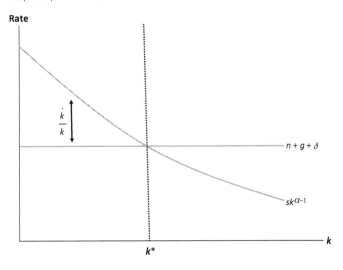

Source: Author's illustration.

state value of capital per effective worker $k*$, the faster k will accelerate or decelerate.

If all economies are assumed to have the same values for n, s, δ, and g, one implication of the Solow model is that economies that are further away from the steady state will grow faster than economies that are closer to the steady state. Eventually, however, all economies will converge to the same steady state rate of growth. This convergence toward a common steady state is known as *absolute convergence*. If the values of n, s, δ, and g differ, economies will experience *conditional convergence*, meaning they will converge with one another conditional on the fact that they have different underlying fundamentals and thus different steady state values of k. When faster growth occurs in one country relative to another because the first country is further from its steady state, such growth is called *catch-up growth*.

The level of output per worker during the transition to a steady state can also be determined.[1] At all times, the level of output per worker is described by

$$\frac{Y_t}{L_t} = \left[\frac{s}{n+g+\delta}(1-e^{-\lambda t}) + k_0^{1-\alpha}e^{-\lambda t} \right]^{\frac{\alpha}{1-\alpha}} A_t, \quad (2.7)$$

where $\lambda = (1-\alpha)(n+g+\delta)$, which is the rate of convergence to the steady state.

Whereas equation (2.6) describes output per worker along the balanced growth path, equation (2.7) describes the *actual* path of output per worker at all points in time. Understanding where the economy is heading means understanding how the actual path of output per worker differs from where it would be along a balanced growth path. To solve for the time it takes an economy to transition halfway to its balanced growth path, the equation $e^{-\lambda t} = 0.5$ need only be solved by plugging in the appropriate values for λ and solving for t. Some empirical estimates put the value of λ at about 0.02,[2] which would imply it takes an economy about 35 years to converge halfway to the steady state. For obvious reasons, this value is known as an economy's *convergence half-life*.

Classification of
Growth Effects

Acentral finding of the Solow model is that permanent changes to the growth rate of output per
worker result only from permanent changes in the
growth rate of technology, *g*. As will be shown here, this
statement is not strictly true. Recurring shocks to other
variables in the model can produce growth rate effects in
the Solow model. For now, however, it is fair to say that the
most straightforward manner by which the growth rate of
output per worker can change permanently in the Solow
model is through permanent shocks to the growth rate of
the technology index, *A* (i.e., changes in *g*). Alternatively,
one could say that permanent changes in the growth rate
of output per worker along a balanced growth path are
caused only by changes in the growth rate of technology.
This distinction is subtle but will become clearer in the
sections that follow.

The variable *g* is exogenous in the Solow model, so
the long-run growth rate of the economy in this model is
actually determined outside the model itself. Permanent
shocks to the other exogenous variables in the Solow
model—the savings rate, the labor force growth rate, and
the depreciation rate of capital—produce *level effects*. When
thinking about the effects of regulations on economic

growth, one should consider which of these key variables are affected (or shocked) by a particular policy and, by extension, what type of corresponding growth effect (level, growth rate, etc.) takes place with respect to output per worker. This distinction between the initial shock and the resulting effect is key to understanding growth changes.

This chapter reviews what is meant by level effects and growth rate effects, with one additional type of change added to the list—*transitory* growth effects. These effects are changes in output per worker that later reverse themselves. As will be shown, there are connections between these three types of changes that make them hard to distinguish in the real world.

First, consider an economy that is operating along a balanced growth path. Such a situation occurs when an economy has reached its steady state level of capital per effective worker in the Solow model. The balanced growth path will change when a key variable in the model is hit by a shock. A shock could be caused by a policy, such as a regulation or a tax, or by other forces, such as an invention, a war, or a natural disaster. Here, shocks are thought of primarily as regulations, but note that other kinds of shocks exist as well.

Shocks change the balanced growth path of an economy, setting output per worker on a new course. The economy will experience transition dynamics until the new balanced growth path is reached, at which time output per worker will grow at a constant rate, determined by the growth rate of technology. Sometimes, the new balanced growth path will be the same as the old one before the shock hit (as is the case following transitory growth effects). Other times, the balanced growth path will be entirely different from the one the economy was on before the shock hit.

The *long run* in our model is defined as the time it takes for an economy to converge to its new balanced growth path after a shock occurs. The *short run* is the transition period after an economy leaves its initial balanced growth path but before it converges to the new balanced growth path. Technically, an economy *never* reaches its new balanced growth path after a shock to a variable in the model. The economy only converges toward its new balanced growth path asymptotically. This convergence should be obvious when one thinks about the half-life equation. Much as nuclear material never completely loses its entire radioactivity, an economy never fully converges to a new balanced growth path. Rather, it gets closer and closer to the balanced growth path without ever reaching it. In this sense, an economy is *always* in the short run. This situation does not mean the long run is not important, however. The long run describes the trajectory the economy is on, and long-run forces are what determine where the economy is heading. Furthermore, at some point, short-run transitional changes become so small that they can be safely disregarded as inconsequential.

GROWTH RATE EFFECT

Figure 3.1, panel a illustrates an economy that begins along a balanced growth path. Initially, all per-effective-worker variables are growing at a rate of 0, and all per-actual-worker variables are growing at a constant rate g. At time t_0, this economy experiences a shock to the

Figure 3.1. Growth Rate Effect

a. Levels

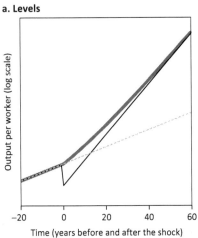

b. Growth rates

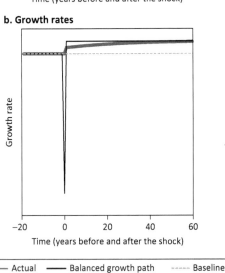

———— Actual   ———— Balanced growth path   - - - - Baseline

Source: Author's illustration, created using DeLong 2006.

variable g in the model.[1] Here the y-axis measures output per worker on a log scale, with time plotted on the x-axis. Levels of output per worker are plotted in log form, so the growth rate of output per worker is simply the slope of the gray line.

The gray line in figure 3.1, panel a represents the actual path of output per worker over time. In year 0, this economy experiences a shock to the variable g. The dotted line shows how the level of output per worker would have continued absent the shock. This dotted line is the *baseline scenario*. Understanding how public policies affect economic growth means understanding how policies change output per worker relative to a baseline scenario. The difference between the gray and dotted lines is the change in output per worker resulting from the shock to g. The black line shows the balanced growth path at all points in time.

Again, it is important to distinguish between the shock itself and the resulting effect of the shock. The shock affects an exogenous variable in the model, whereas the resulting growth effect will be reflected in changes in output per worker. Sometimes shocks will be temporary, and other times they will be permanent. The same goes for changes in output per worker. Sometimes the effect will be temporary and other times permanent.

In the case of figure 3.1, panel a, a permanent shock to the variable g in the Solow model permanently affects the path of output per worker. At the time of the shock, the balanced growth path and the actual path of output per worker diverge. To understand why this happens, take the logarithm of both sides of equation (2.6) to obtain

$$ln\left(\frac{Y_t}{L_t}\right) = ln A_0 + gt + \frac{\alpha}{1-\alpha}ln(s)$$
$$-\frac{\alpha}{1-\alpha}ln(n-g-\delta). \qquad (3.1)$$

The variable g exerts influence on the log of the balanced growth path of output per worker in two ways. First, g changes the level of the technology index, A. Next, g changes the level of break-even investment of capital per effective worker. A higher g implies a higher level of break-even investment, meaning more capital is needed to offset new and better technology just to keep capital per effective worker constant.

The first effect of g raises output per worker, and the second effect depresses output per worker. In the very short run, this downward *level effect* of g actually outweighs the *growth rate effect* that g exerts by raising A. Figure 3.1, panel b illustrates this effect more clearly by plotting the growth rates associated with the lines in figure 3.1, panel a.

Although the initial effect of an increase in g is to put downward pressure on output per worker, the effect is quickly swamped by the upward pressure that g exerts on the level of A. The capital stock of an economy cannot immediately jump to its new balanced growth path because the capital stock is fixed in the short term. Because it takes time to adjust to the shock, once the capital stock starts to adjust, the upward growth rate effect of g outweighs downward-level pressures.

Permanent changes in the growth rate of technology have radical implications over time. Such changes result in revolutions—for better or worse—in living standards. When the growth rate of output per worker changes permanently, the laws of compounding take hold and the gap between the actual level of output per worker and the level of output per worker under the baseline scenario widens by a greater and greater amount over time.

What kinds of things might induce such effects? The growth rate of GDP per person has actually remained remarkably steady over time, at about 2 percent per year in the United States since the late 19th century (C. I. Jones 2015). Similar evidence can be presented for other advanced economies. The lack of any significant variation in the long-run intensive growth rate is an important empirical finding when considering how public policies, such as regulation, affect growth rates. Growth appears to be fairly resistant to policy changes, at least over the very long run. Over shorter time horizons, growth rates vary widely, however. In the past 60 years, US growth rates in real GDP per capita have been as high as 11 percent in some years and as low as –4 percent in others, as is demonstrated in figure 3.2. Business cycles are a main reason for this variation, but one has to wonder whether policy might have contributed to these wide swings as well.

For a policy to affect long-run growth rates, it must permanently change the productivity growth rate in the Solow model. Any single policy is unlikely to do this, although it is conceivable that the cumulative effect of many policies might impact productivity in this way. New discoveries or inventions might also permanently raise the productivity growth rate of workers. However, most inventions will increase only the *level* of the technology index, A, in the Solow model. Only technologies with sweeping, economy-wide effects could conceivably raise g permanently, and such technologies are likely to be incredibly rare, if they exist at all.

Figure 3.2. US Real GDP per Capita Growth Rates, 1948–2015

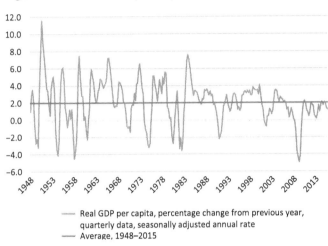

Real GDP per capita, percentage change from previous year, quarterly data, seasonally adjusted annual rate
Average, 1948–2015

Source: Author's illustration, based on data from the US Bureau of Economic Analysis 2016.

The only technologies that might come close to having such effects are general purpose technologies (GPTs), which have been defined in many ways.[2] In this book, the definition in Lipsey, Bekar, and Carlaw (2005, 98) is used: "A GPT is a single generic technology, recognizable as such over its whole lifetime, that initially has much scope for improvement and eventually comes to be widely used, to have many uses, and to have many spillover effects." Jovanovic and Rousseau (2005), who build on the work of Bresnahan and Trajtenberg (1995), suggest that GPTs have three main features: (a) *pervasiveness*—the GPT should spread to most sectors; (b) *improvement*—the GPT should get better over time and, hence, should keep lowering the costs of its users; and (c) *innovation spawning*—the GPT should make it easier to invent and produce new products or processes.

For a single technology to permanently raise the growth rate of all technologies, it must have endless uses. For a GPT to do so, it must be broad enough that it leads to further innovations in other areas. Perhaps the best example of a technology such as this is electricity. Society seems to never run out of new ways to use electricity, and without electricity there would not be other GPTs, such as computers or the Internet. Historical examples of GPTs are given in table 3.1.

It is hard to say whether any regulations have prevented the discovery, invention, or widespread adoption of a GPT. Even if this has occurred, it's unclear whether this has reduced the growth rate significantly in developed economies. Nonetheless, just because growth has been fairly stable in the recent past does not mean it will be stable in the future. During most of the time that the human race has been on Earth, per capita income growth has been closer to 0 percent. Only since the Industrial Revolution have developed countries experienced per capita income growth on the order of 2 percent per year, suggesting that no one should assume that annual increases in living standards are automatic. This fact suggests that policymakers should be careful about blocking or delaying implementation of new technologies—especially if the technologies have the potential to be GPTs. Even short delays in the adoption rate of technologies that permanently raise productivity can have permanent effects. As an illustration, figure 3.3 shows how a delayed growth rate effect compares against a world in which there is no delay.

The black line plots output per worker when a permanent increase in the productivity growth rate occurs in year 0. The gray line plots what happens if the change occurs 20 years later. As the graph makes clear, the

Table 3.1. Historical Examples of General Purpose Technologies

No.	GPT	Date
1	Domestication of plants	9000–8000 BC
2	Domestication of animals	8500–7500 BC
3	Smelting ore	8000–7000 BC
4	Wheel	4000–3000 BC
5	Writing	3400–3200 BC
6	Bronze	2800 BC
7	Iron	1200 BC
8	Waterwheel	Early medieval period
9	Three-masted sailing ship	15th century
10	Printing	16th century
11	Steam engine	Late 18th to early 19th century
12	Factory system	Late 18th to early 19th century
13	Railway	Mid-19th century
14	Iron steamship	Mid-19th century
15	Internal combustion engine	Late 19th century
16	Electricity	Late 19th century
17	Motor vehicle	20th century
18	Airplane	20th century
19	Mass-production, continuous-process factory	20th century
20	Computer	20th century
21	Lean production	20th century
22	Internet	20th century
23	Biotechnology	20th century
24	Nanotechnology	21st century

Note: GPT = general purpose technology.
Source: Lipsey, Bekar, and Carlaw 2005.

Figure 3.3. Immediate vs. Delayed Growth Rate Effect

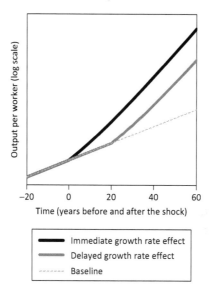

Source: Author's illustration, created using DeLong 2006.

effects of any delay are permanent. Every year, every day, even every minute that goes by without the technological breakthrough lowers the level of output per worker permanently.

There are also important redistributive consequences of growth rate effects. Technological innovations that are disruptive are likely to be heavily resisted when introduced, especially by interest groups that might be harmed or displaced by change. The Luddites, British textile workers who feared the new textile equipment that was developed during the Industrial Revolution, are a famous example of an interest group that was displaced by a beneficial new technology. In retrospect, their concerns seem almost comical. But in the emotion of the moment and to those who are affected directly, concern about disruptive technological change is legitimate.

Interest groups, as well as the public more broadly, often initially respond more powerfully to the negative aspects of new technologies than to the positive aspects. In part, this may be because of the psychological phenomenon of loss aversion (i.e., people tend to respond more strongly to losses than to equivalent gains), but resistance could also be a rational response to incentives created by technological change. If new technologies are disruptive at first and the benefits come mostly later on, the harms of new technologies fall on the present generation, and the greatest beneficiaries are future generations. No doubt, new technologies also benefit people in the present, but the compounding effects of productivity improvements will be most profound years into the future.

The kinds of sweeping, dramatic growth rate effects described here may be more the domain of theory than practice. It is unlikely that any single policy, unless it prevents or encourages a massive technological revolution, can influence economic growth rates in the manner described above. Even most GPTs probably do not raise economic growth rates permanently, although models do exist that explain growth as driven by a single GPT.[3] The consistency of growth rates over time is further evidence of this. Nonetheless, volatility in short-run growth rates suggests that regulatory policy may still be important. The most likely way is by changing the level of output per worker, and by extension the economy's short-run growth rate.

LEVEL EFFECT

Standard Level Effects

This section discusses two forms of *level effects*, which occur when the level of output per worker along a balanced growth path is permanently shifted higher or lower. Unlike growth rate effects that compound over time, a level effect changes the level of output per worker by a uniform amount in every period once a new balanced growth path is reached. Such effects are caused by permanent shocks to the variables n, s, or δ in the Solow model. Here, changes produced by permanent shocks to these variables are referred to as *standard level effects* to distinguish them from temporary shocks to technology, which also induce level effects and which will be discussed in the second half of this section.

Level effects do not compound over time like growth rate effects. Instead, they produce fixed (positive or negative) changes in long-run output per worker indefinitely into the future. Figure 3.4, panel a illustrates a positive level effect on output per worker.

Although level effects do not change an economy's growth rate in the long run, they do change growth rates during transition periods before an economy reaches its new balanced growth path. Initially, an economy's growth rate rises after a positive level effect; then growth slowly returns to its original level; and in the long run, the growth rate remains what it was before the shock occurred, as shown in figure 3.4, panel b.

In the Solow model, several types of shocks can induce standard level effects: a permanent shock to the labor force growth rate n, a permanent shock to the savings rate s, or a permanent change in the depreciation rate of capital δ.

Figure 3.4. Standard Level Effect

a. Levels

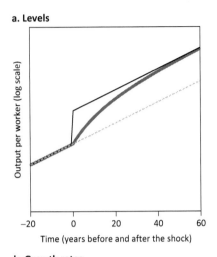

b. Growth rates

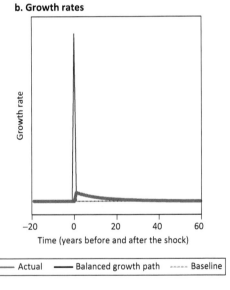

——— Actual ——— Balanced growth path ----- Baseline

Source: Author's illustrations, created using DeLong 2006.

Any regulation that influences these variables permanently will produce a level effect. From a policy standpoint, several factors might influence the labor force growth rate n. For instance, some regulations might indirectly affect the population's fertility rate. Legalized abortion, for example, might have this effect. Public pension programs may discourage couples from having children (as individuals learn they can rely on other people's children to support them in old age rather than their own). Alternatively, other policies, such as a child tax credit, might incentivize families to have even more children.

Stricter immigration restrictions would raise output per worker in the Solow model if it slowed labor force growth. Yet other policies, such as unemployment insurance or disability insurance, might encourage people to stay out of the labor force altogether. All else equal, if the fraction of people working in the population falls, this would raise output *per worker*. But such a decline in working might also lower output *per capita*, because the total population hasn't changed. Everyone is now supported by fewer workers.

These population-related outcomes from the model might be counterintuitive, but the reasoning is simple. The Solow model assumes diminishing returns to production factors, so anything that increases the number of workers along a balanced growth path will reduce output per worker. In this way, population growth is a fairly negative development in the Solow model. It might even be viewed as a Malthusian result of the model, after the classical economist Thomas Malthus, who also had a fairly pessimistic view of how the size of a population affects living standards. As will be shown in chapter 5, however, not all growth models share this pessimistic perspective about the relationship between the size of the population and living standards.

For a policy to result in a level effect, the change must be strong enough to alter the growth rate, not just the level, of the labor force. (Policies that change only the level of the labor force are relevant to transitory growth effects and are discussed later in this chapter.) A significant policy, or set of policies, will be needed to create this change. Such policies, if they exist, will relate primarily to immigration and fertility, topics largely outside the scope of this book. Similarly, the depreciation rate of capital, δ, will be assumed to be determined by factors mostly unrelated to public policy, although the rate of innovation may spill over and affect how quickly capital depreciates.

It is far more likely that regulations induce level effects by influencing s through changes in consumption and investment behavior. For example, policies that prompt individuals to contribute more to their 401(k) accounts might increase the national savings rate if the added savings are not offset by less investment elsewhere. Alternatively, restrictions on investments of various kinds might discourage people from saving and thereby reduce output per worker. Financial regulations are likely to be particularly important given their direct effects on various types of investment.

As with growth rate effects, important distributional factors must be considered with level effects. Because the gap between long-run output per worker and output per worker under the baseline scenario is constant over time, an immediate level effect that reduces output per worker by \$1,000 today will also reduce output per worker by \$1,000 next year, the year after, and so on. If incomes are rising over time, the change will feel far more significant today than it will in the future. Even adjusted for inflation, \$1,000 may feel relatively inconsequential as a fraction of income to an American 100 years from now. As a fraction of this year's median income, \$1,000 is quite significant.

Because of this distributional effect, policies that produce positive level effects can be expected to have progressive redistributive consequences across time in the sense that the policies provide gains that are a larger fraction of income to the present poorer generation than to future richer generations. Policies that produce negative level effects have regressive redistributive consequences. In either case, level effects will seem to be of more consequence to people in the present than to people in the future, assuming that income levels are higher in the future. This distributional consequence is an important contrast between growth rate effects and level effects. Growth rate effects produce consequences that will feel most pronounced in the future. Given their attention to short-run factors, it may well be policymakers and voters alike are more concerned with producing positive level effects and avoiding negative level effects than they are with policies that produce growth rate effects.

Technology-Induced Level Effects

Temporary shocks to g in the Solow model also produce level effects. Such an outcome is almost identical to the level effects produced by permanent shocks to n, s, or δ, although the transition path that the level of output-per-worker follows is not identical in the two cases. Figure 3.5 illustrates such technology-induced level effects. A technology shock arrives at time t_0, lasts for one year, and then abruptly reverses.

One can imagine temporary shocks to g, such as those presented in figure 3.5, occurring for many reasons. First, a powerful new technology might get started but then never fully take off. If some critical mass of use is necessary before people fully adopt a new technology, such a technology might begin to increase productivity, but then the change could reverse if the technology falls out of favor. Technologies often have a life cycle that eventually runs out, as well. Consider a simple fax machine, which initially improved business productivity because it reduced the time required to send documents long distances. Over time, however, marginal uses of the facsimile (such as spamming by marketers) likely did not add much value. Eventually, with the advent of email, fax machines became largely obsolete.

Most technologies—maybe even most GPTs—experience diminishing returns. With diminishing returns, new discoveries will not induce *permanent* technology shocks but instead *temporary* shocks, which result in level effects and not growth rate effects. In most cases, it is reasonable to think that shocks to g are temporary, not permanent.

In the Solow model, technological improvements are basically a catchall term for anything that improves productivity. It has been well documented that regulations often affect the productivity of firms in a negative manner.[4] This result is fairly straightforward. Regulations create added costs for firms. Those regulations may have benefits,

Figure 3.5. Technology-Induced Level Effect

a. Levels

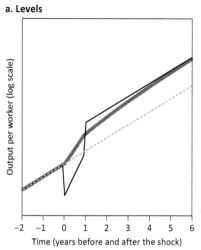

b. Growth rates

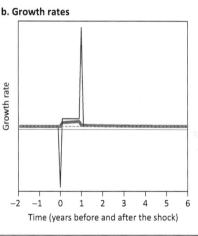

Source: Author's illustrations, created using DeLong 2006.

but typically the intended benefits are not to increase firm output. Rather, as managers and employees devote time to understanding and complying with regulations, the cost per unit of output increases. Hence, by definition, the productivity of the firm is lowered as output per unit of input declines.

Some regulations induce laborers to work harder, thereby boosting productivity. For example, minimum wage laws can have the side effect of causing workers who retain their jobs to work harder. Wages that are above the market-clearing wage can boost employee morale, prevent shirking, and lower turnover costs for firms (Yellen 1984). The existence of structural unemployment caused by minimum wage laws might also increase worker productivity as workers fear being cast into the ranks of the unemployed and work harder as a result. Of course, it is unclear whether such policies will actually increase output per worker because fewer workers are employed overall, a result that highlights how productivity and output per worker can move in opposite directions. Such policies also create winners and losers, so it is ambiguous whether social welfare is improved.

Another interesting implication of level effects is what happens when they are delayed. Consider when a new productivity-boosting technology comes around. A delay in adopting it will make no difference to output per worker in the long run. This result is shown in figure 3.6, which illustrates a level effect that takes place at time t_0, compared against the same effect after a 10-year delay. With or without a delay, as long as the technology is eventually adopted and the technology experiences diminishing returns, output per worker will look the same in the long run under both scenarios.

Figure 3.6. Immediate vs. Delayed Level Effect

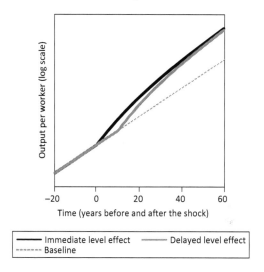

Source: Author's illustration, created using DeLong 2006.

Recall from figure 3.3 that delaying a beneficial growth rate change leads to permanent losses in income. If a policy were to cause this effect, it would have devastating consequences. As figure 3.6 demonstrates, however, a counterproductive policy producing a negative level effect can be reversed with no long-run effect. This result suggests that level effects are often reversible, whereas growth rate effects are not. This is true for policies that produce both positive and negative outcomes.

These findings are relevant to the *precautionary principle* in public policy. That principle has been described as "the belief that new innovations should be curtailed or disallowed until their developers can prove that they will not cause any harms to individuals, groups, specific entities, cultural norms, or various existing laws, norms, or traditions" (Thierer 2016, 1).

Advocates of the precautionary principle argue for delaying new technologies until they are proven safe. This approach to policy will influence economic growth very differently depending on the type of technology being affected. With sweeping revolutionary technologies, such as some GPTs, a huge tradeoff may be required if the precautionary principle is taken seriously. Even if a technology has the potential to result in catastrophic outcomes (e.g., nuclear power), delaying adoption of a new GPT could also have catastrophic outcomes to living standards.

With smaller innovations or with technologies that are expected to run into diminishing returns eventually, the precautionary principle has lower opportunity costs. Delays in small innovations will make little difference to output in the longer run. But this result does not mean there are no consequences of delay. Rather, for less consequential technologies, the relative benefits and costs of each new technology must be carefully weighed when making judgment calls about how quickly to adopt. Upfront risks must be balanced against the benefits of a new technology, keeping in mind that it is the present generation of citizens that will realize the benefits most profoundly.

If the potential exists for large catastrophic consequences from a small or diminishing-returns new technology, delaying the technology may be a sensible idea until more is known. However, if the downside risks are small and the technology is likely to bring much utility to the current generation, delay does not make as much sense. Furthermore, a permanent delay, such as banning a technology, results in permanent losses regardless of whether the technology would produce level or growth rate effects.

Therefore, the precautionary principle should be taken seriously, but along a continuum. The shorter the implementation delay, the more limited the potential applications of a new technology (i.e., the less pervasive, the less room for improvement in the technology, and the less innovation-spawning the technology is likely to be), the higher the downside risks, the more the precautionary principle might be reasonable. By contrast, the longer the delay is likely to be, the more wide-ranging and applicable the new technology is (i.e., the more it is like a GPT), and the lower the downside risks, the more the precautionary principle is unreasonable.

TRANSITORY GROWTH EFFECT

The final type of change discussed here is a *transitory growth effect*, which results from a temporary shock to n, s, or δ that eventually reverses. Transitory effects do not change output per worker in the long run; rather, their effects eventually wither and slowly disappear.

If the labor force growth rate increases in a single year and then returns to its previous rate, this would produce the type of effect seen in figure 3.7. A sudden burst in immigration might temporarily boost the growth rate of the country's labor force. If, after a year, the growth of the labor force returns to its previous rate,[5] then in the long run, output per worker will return to the same balanced growth path as before the burst. Something similar would occur if the growth rate of the capital stock were to fall suddenly once. The transition dynamics are such that the growth rate initially turns negative before

Figure 3.7. Transitory Growth Effects

a. Levels

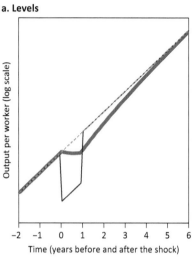

Output per worker (log scale)

Time (years before and after the shock)

b. Growth rate

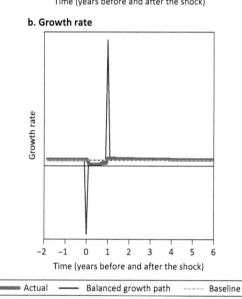

Growth rate

Time (years before and after the shock)

Actual —— Balanced growth path ⋯⋯ Baseline

Source: Author's illustrations, created using DeLong 2006.

balancing off, speeding up, and ultimately returning to its initial rate.

As with level effects, delaying transitory growth effects will not matter in the long run. Output is eventually no different than if the effect never occurred. Nonetheless, short-run effects such as these can be very large in magnitude, and their effects can last for years owing to the long convergence half-life found in most economies. Most recessions are examples of transitory growth effects, and few would argue that recessions have no meaningful consequences. Furthermore, delaying a transitory growth effect will have important distributional consequences. A shock that occurs today will affect a different group of people than a shock that occurs 10 years from now. Even if in the long run such effects do not matter much, they can matter a great deal to the people who are directly affected.

Because regulations govern the flows of both global capital and migration, regulations can indeed produce such effects, and the types of regulations that induce transitory growth effects mirror many of those that produce standard level effects. The only difference is whether the shock caused by the regulation is temporary or permanent. For example, if rules that encourage firms to invest abroad are suddenly repealed, a flood of investment might rush back into the country in a very short period of time. There would be a temporary investment boom that would later reverse itself, as eventually investment would return to its usual level.

These findings also have relevance to the expenditures made by firms when engaging in compliance activities. Recurring compliance costs that displace investment by firms, such as the ongoing costs of maintaining compliance departments, will lead to downward level shifts in output per worker. Yet one-off drops in investment, such as the one-time cost of a government information collection request, will produce transitory effects. Some policies will produce a short-run transitory boom followed by a longer-run bust. For example, the 2009 "cash for clunkers" car exchange program[6] likely caused consumers to shift purchases of vehicles forward in time at the expense of future expenditures.

Of course, astute observers will note that many compliance expenditures actually show up in GDP because filling out forms and having lawyers draw up documents are both market activities. It is debatable whether compliance activities should be included in GDP. Remember, GDP measures the market value of final goods and services, and compliance expenditures look a lot like spending on intermediate goods where the *final* good consumed by the public is whatever outcome the compliance activity is intended to bring about. If a plant installs pollution control equipment, the final good consumed by the public is cleaner air, not the pollution control equipment. The final good—cleaner air—is like a good that is sold to the public at zero price.

Recall that GDP is not a measure of overall human well-being; rather, it is a measure of income, which is related to well-being but is not the same thing. Although clean air provides benefits to the public, it does not directly contribute to national income. Thus, a more accurate measure of national income might exclude compliance expenditures from GDP and treat them more as something along the lines of charity. Although this exclusion may at first sound controversial, it should not be. It is simply an example of how income and welfare do not always move in the same direction.

It is also important to distinguish between (a) output losses resulting from declines in investment and (b) any additional losses resulting from productivity declines as a firm's attention is diverted from production activities and toward compliance activities. Compliance activities can affect s and g simultaneously as businesses (a) reduce investment when they are forced to spend resources on compliance and (b) suffer productivity losses as effort is diverted from production activity. Keeping these different shocks and outcomes distinct is critical. To assist in this endeavor, chapter 4 explores more formally how regulatory shocks can influence multiple variables in a growth model at the same time.

INTERRELATIONS OF GROWTH EFFECTS

Shocks to individual variables in the Solow model can produce very different types of changes, depending on whether a given shock is permanent or temporary. Similarly, the different kinds of growth effects can be viewed as recurring or one-time versions of other effects. For example, a level effect can be viewed as a series of permanently recurring transitory growth effects. This relationship is illustrated in figure 3.8. Level effects occur when temporary shocks occur every period in perpetuity, each one producing a transitory growth effect. The black lines in figure 3.8 show the balanced growth paths associated with each new shock; the gray line represents the actual path of output per worker as the economy is subjected to a series of permanently recurring transitory growth effects.

Because of this relationship between transitory growth effects and level effects, it might be inferred that growth

Figure 3.8. Recurring Transitory Growth Effects

a. Levels

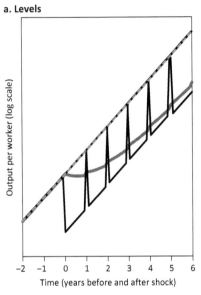

b. Growth rates

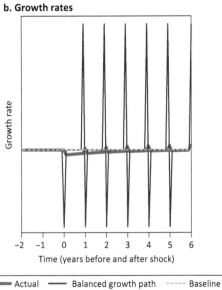

〰 Actual — Balanced growth path 〰〰 Baseline

Source: Author's illustrations, created using DeLong 2006.

rate effects can be thought of as a series of permanently recurring level effects, which indeed turns out to be the case. Recurring, and permanent, shocks to the variables n, s, or δ in the Solow model produce growth rate effects when the shocks build on one another. Thus, the variables that are sometimes claimed to produce "only" level effects in the Solow model—n, s, or δ—can actually produce growth rate effects as well. To do so, however, shocks to these variables must permanently prevent the economy from reaching its balanced growth path, as shown in figure 3.9. For example, a series of unrelated temporary shocks to productivity could result in a growth rate effect.

Of course, permanently recurring rises or declines in population growth, the savings rate, or the depreciation rate are difficult to achieve on an ongoing basis. A society cannot save more than 100 percent or less than 0 percent of its income, so it is impossible to permanently increase the savings rate by 1 percent each year in perpetuity. People would have to stop eating at some point. That said, small changes in these three rates are realistic, and the effects could last for years or decades—such that what actually is a level effect feels permanent and feels like a growth rate effect, even if at some point the economy eventually reaches its balanced growth path. The lesson here is that it is the cumulative effect of a series of public policies—many completely unrelated—that will induce growth rate effects most often. And this will happen through simultaneous and recurring shocks to investment and productivity. A single policy in isolation will rarely achieve such an outcome.

Figure 3.9. Recurring Level Effects

a. Levels

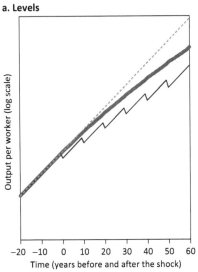

b. Growth rates

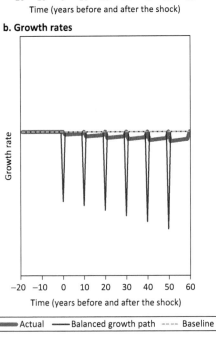

Actual ▬▬▬ Balanced growth path ▬▬▬ Baseline ▭▭▭

Source: Author's illustrations, created using DeLong 2006.

4

How Regulations Enter the Economic System

O ne reason the cumulative effect of all regulations together may have the most consequences with respect to growth rates is that new regulations interact with existing ones, resulting in effects larger than the new regulations would create on their own. Consider the simple case where there are only two rules on the books— one old and one new. Both regulations might have an effect on production when acting in isolation, but there is also the potential for an interaction effect between the two regulations once both are in place at the same time.

Interaction effects among regulations have been compared to dropping pebbles in a stream (Mandel and Carew 2013). The first pebble may not slow the flow of water in a noticeable way, but the thousandth pebble might, and the millionth pebble might stop the flow altogether. This example is true despite the fact that the millionth pebble might be of little consequence if it were the first pebble dropped in the water. When hundreds of thousands of requirements are on the books, adding a single new one can produce much larger effects than one would expect from looking at that regulation in isolation.

Anticipating the possible interaction effects of so many rules is a daunting task. The task becomes ever more difficult when considering how the effects of regulations change over time. A regulation issued in period t will have effects in periods $t + 1$, $t + 2$, and so forth. Interaction effects of the regulation may differ in every period. Regulations may even interact with themselves across time, a phenomenon known as *serial correlation*.

One implication of interaction effects is that added complexity itself may induce changes in output per worker, although such effects are poorly understood. If one is inclined to think that greater complexity is more likely to lower rather than increase output per worker, this provides a rationale for capping the size of the regulatory code at some manageable level. One way to achieve this would be to remove an old requirement every time a new one is put in place to ensure the code does not grow over time.

Microeconomic analysis will probably not be able to estimate the cumulative effects of regulatory complexity, but macroeconomists may have more success. Indeed, macroeconomists have already begun looking at the cumulative effect of all regulations on growth, and the results are profound. One study finds that the cumulative burden of regulations has slowed the growth rate of GDP in the United States by approximately 2 percent every year since 1949 (Dawson and Seater 2013). The same study finds that regulations also affect other key growth determinants, such as total factor productivity and capital and labor services. A clear lesson is that regulators should be ever more careful as more and more rules continue to be put in place, because there are likely to be additional unintended consequences as the code grows larger.

THE INNOVATION SPIDER WEB

Regulations restrict behavior and limit the range of opportunities available to people. This constraining aspect of regulation is why some recent measures of regulation count restrictions—words such as *prohibited* and *may not*—that appear in the US regulatory code. As of this writing, more than 1 million restrictions are found in the *US Code of Federal Regulations* (Al-Ubaydli and McLaughlin 2015). Limiting choices can be beneficial if some choices would result in undesirable harms. However, restricting choice prevents beneficial outcomes from transpiring as well.

From a growth perspective, the most important beneficial outcomes will be innovations that enhance worker productivity. In the Solow model, such an improvement would be anything that raises the level of the technology index, A. The models reviewed in chapter 5 will show how productivity enhancements through innovation can come in many forms: formal education and job training, informal learning through work experience and specialization, new products and capital goods, quality improvements, and knowledge transfer and imitation.

Formal education and training includes, for example, completing a course in computer programming to learn new skills. By contrast, informal learning through experience or specialization takes place when, for example, a worker on an assembly line learns how to make finicky machinery run smoothly. Both innovations might increase daily output at a factory, even with no new labor or capital added to the production process. New products increase both the number of goods and services that consumers may purchase and the number of capital goods available to produce more consumer goods. Quality improvements occur when an old product, such as a rotary telephone, is replaced with a new and better version—the smartphone. Finally, knowledge transfer and imitation occur through the sharing of information. For example, when a US company opens a factory in China, plant managers might teach the new employees methods of production that were developed in the United States.

Because innovations come in all shapes and sizes, it may seem odd to lump them together in one category. There is also likely to be some overlap in the categories described here. The one characteristic all these innovations have in common, however, is that they increase productivity. Furthermore, many such enhancements relate to the discovery and use of knowledge. Sometimes newly discovered knowledge is just that: it has never been known to another human being. More often, however, knowledge exists in certain times and places and must be rediscovered or transferred to new individuals to be put to good use. The diffusion of knowledge is what enhances productivity, drives economic growth, and raises living standards.

Regulation can play an important role in both advancing and stifling knowledge diffusion. Knowledge can be thought of as existing in a kind of innovation spider web, whereby discoveries are mapped according to the pathways that allow individuals to uncover new productivity-enhancing information. Figure 4.1 provides an illustration of the innovation spider web. The black lines represent the various paths by which discoveries can be made, and the gray circles are the innovations themselves. Restrictions limit the number of discovery pathways that are available to society. In extreme cases, these restrictions make it impossible for specific innovations to be uncovered.

Figure 4.1. Innovation Spider Web

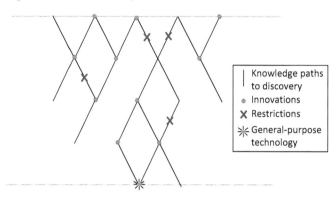

Key:

| Knowledge paths to discovery
● Innovations
✗ Restrictions
✳ General-purpose technology

Source: Author's illustration.

Of course, it is not always bad if some innovations are sealed off and kept out of reach. Most people would not want to see innovations that lead to low-priced portable nuclear weapons. Such an innovation might increase the productivity of terrorists, but not all productivity is good. Unfortunately, if society restricts discovery pathways, it can never be sure if access is being blocked to only harmful innovations or also beneficial discoveries. This predicament is the very nature of undiscovered knowledge.

Restrictions that block discovery paths need not be regulations, either. Culture and religion restrict behavior as well, and such restrictions can also block discovery pathways. The printing press, invented in the 1400s, met resistance from some leaders in the Roman Catholic Church in Western Europe and Islamic leaders in the Middle East. Countries with greater openness to technological change have generally thrived economically compared with those that resist and reject technological change (Comin, Easterly, and Gong 2010).

Even market prices, which are often a useful guide for entrepreneurs looking to buy low and sell high, can be remarkably deceptive when it comes to innovations. Market prices will not reflect the opportunity cost of resources if some uses of those resources are not yet known. For example, before the many uses for oil were discovered, the commodity was likely viewed as useless sludge. Prices reflect only information that is known to people, but when people do not possess certain kinds of information, prices can be misleading.

Aside from regulations, other forms of law, such as patent protections, also can restrict pathways to innovation. In some extreme cases, patent protections have led to what is known as the *tragedy of the anticommons* (Heller 1998). The tragedy of the anticommons occurs when multiple parties own rights to the same resource, such as when multiple government authorities have the taxing power to install tolls on a road. This overlapping of rights can lead to underuse of resources.

In the case of patents, the tragedy of the anticommons plays out as a fragmentation of the market (Boldrin and Levine 2008). If different parties hold the rights to unique knowledge pathways along the spider web of innovations, the resulting scenario is that no one has the ability to reach certain innovations without first gaining the consent of many other parties. A coordination problem exists because the transaction costs involved in gaining the consent of every unique patent holder can exceed the expected returns of discoveries. The benefit-cost calculus an entrepreneur faces may make innovation not worth the cost of obtaining permission, even if the benefits would vastly outweigh the costs in a world where innovation could occur without permission.

In such cases, fewer innovations will be developed than is socially desirable. A scenario such as this may even be occurring in the United States now. There have been significant increases in the number of patents granted in recent years (Dourado and Tabarrok 2015), even as productivity growth remains relatively low compared with historical averages. It might be that either (a) these patents protect inventions that do not have much productivity-enhancing effect or (b) the patents themselves are stifling productivity growth by granting excessive monopoly privileges rather than encouraging innovation.

SPECIALIZATION AND THE EXTENT OF THE MARKET

Usually, when regulations block access to new innovations, the innovations in question probably have a narrow range of highly specific uses, as opposed to being general-purpose technologies, which are very rare (at most occurring a few times in a century). Smaller innovations will be more targeted. As a result, it might be surmised that preventing society from having access to smaller discoveries might have limited repercussions, but that is not necessarily the case. Blocking highly specific technologies with narrow uses can still result in significant social losses when whole classes of products or production techniques are prevented from being developed.

One of the interesting aspects about the present age is that production processes tend to require more and more highly specific inputs over time. This fact is simply a characteristic of technological progress. As production becomes ever more complex, inputs in the production process become more highly specialized, which is true of inputs such as workers and also of equipment that may be perfectly tailored for a particular task. In complex processes, a single missing or faulty element in the production chain can cause the entire production line to fail. This situation has come to be known as the *O-ring theory of economic development* (Kremer 1993a), so named because the 1986 explosion of the *Challenger* was due to failure of the space shuttle's O-rings.

Few would have guessed that one small component, O-rings, in such a complex piece of machinery as a space shuttle could be so critical, but this phenomenon is true in all kinds of production processes. An automobile is useless without brakes. A personal computer is useless without a memory card. As a result, preventing even small, highly specific innovations from being developed can have widespread ripple effects if entire lines of production depend on that small innovation as a critical input.

A key insight from trade theory in recent decades has been that open trade gives firms access to a greater variety of more highly specialized production inputs. Access to such resources allows firms greater opportunity to specialize and differentiate their products. Firms and, indeed, whole industries may face increasing returns to scale for just these kinds of reasons (Krugman 1980). Therefore, regulations in the form of trade restrictions have limited the ability of firms to specialize and to take advantage of increasing returns to scale where it exists.

The focus of this chapter has largely been on how knowledge is the key ingredient to enhancing productivity. Regulations place limits on what kind of knowledge can be discovered, but regulations also affect knowledge generation through changes in investment activity. Chapter 5 looks more closely at how changes in saving and investment contribute to economic growth, and also seeks to explain how knowledge is generated. In the jargon of economists, key variables such as the savings rate and the level of technology will be endogenized in the models reviewed. Previously, these parameters were treated as given. In this way, a deeper analysis is possible of the fundamental causes of economic growth than the Solow model has thus far allowed.

5
Models of Economic Growth

As insightful and influential as the Solow model has been over the past half-century, the model is too simplistic to explain some of the most important aspects of economic growth. The central force behind long-run growth in the Solow model—technology—is determined exogenously. This result is not satisfactory. Over the past few decades, economists have worked with the Solow model's core insights to build more sophisticated models that go further in explaining the most important drivers of growth.

Perhaps the second-most famous growth model in economics is one that brought together the work of Ramsey (1928), Cass (1965), and Koopmans (1965)—aptly named the Ramsey–Cass–Koopmans growth model. Most of the key takeaways from the model mirror those from the Solow model. For example, along a balanced growth path, output per worker grows at rate g, the exogenously determined rate of technological progress. The major difference between the Solow model and the Ramsey–Cass–Koopmans model is that the latter is built on microfoundations. Whereas the Solow model focuses on economy-wide aggregates, such as the national savings rate, the savings rate in the Ramsey–Cass–Koopmans model is endogenously determined as a result of optimization behavior at the individual (or household) level. Specifically, individuals optimize utility, such that their consumption is described according to the function

$$\frac{\dot{c}_t}{c_t} = \frac{r_t - \rho}{\theta}, \qquad (5.1)$$

which states that the consumption path of the representative agent grows at a rate that adjusts to account for the gap between the interest rate r at time t and the agent's rate of time preference, ρ, taking into account the agent's degree of relative risk aversion, θ. Consumption is a *control variable* in the model in that it is the variable that the optimizing agent controls to bring about equilibrium. Both ρ and θ are important new variables in the framework because they help determine the degree to which the representative agent is willing to save and invest.

As in the Solow model, permanent changes in the savings rate still affect the level of output per worker along a balanced growth path, but now there is a microeconomic explanation for what causes a change in the savings rate. A permanent rise in time preference, ρ, means that the representative agent becomes more impatient. Compared to before the change, the agent values present consumption relatively more than future consumption and will shift consumption forward in time accordingly. The national savings rate falls as a result, producing a downward level effect. Thus, shocks to the parameter ρ in the Ramsey–Cass–Koopmans model have effects similar to shocks to s in the Solow model. Permanent shocks to ρ produce level effects, and temporary shocks produce transitory growth effects.

The same is true for the coefficient θ, which explains how risk averse the representative agent is. Theta describes how much risk the agent is willing to bear and also the degree to which the agent's marginal utility declines as consumption rises. A rise in θ means the agent becomes more risk averse and is thus less willing to undergo swings in consumption to take advantage of the gap between the interest rate, r, and the agent's rate of time preference, ρ. A higher θ causes the agent to save less as the agent smooths consumption more across time. This pushes down the level of saving and investment and decreases the level of output per worker.

It is certainly plausible that some regulations might induce the public to be more shortsighted than it might be otherwise. Policies that create principal-agent or moral hazard problems might influence ρ and θ. For example, if managers at firms expect to be bailed out if they get into trouble, these managers might be willing to take on more risk than is optimal and to have less concern for the future. It is more likely that policies influence the rate of return in equation (5.1), however. For example, government borrowing might drive up interest rates, or taxes on investments might drive a wedge between the rate of return earned on investments and the rate of borrowing to pay for the investments. Regulations that change the rate of return on financial assets will influence the consumption behavior described in equation (5.1). In other words, optimizing individuals will adjust their saving and consumption as interest rates move closer or further away from the rate of individuals' time preference.

HUMAN CAPITAL MODELS

In the Solow model, technology augments human labor so as to make it more productive, thus making technology the primary determinant of rising wages. Many economists believe that human capital, which broadly refers to people's knowledge, education, and skills, can also augment labor so as to make it more productive. Human capital is the first form of knowledge that will enter the models reviewed here. One can think of human capital as having previously been included in the technology index, A, and now its effects will be isolated from other labor-augmenting influences. A strong correlation between the level of human capital and GDP per capita across countries provides empirical evidence that the contribution of human capital to growth is meaningful.

The two most famous attempts to incorporate human capital into an economic growth model are from Lucas (1988) and Mankiw, Romer, and Weil (1992). These two models take slightly different approaches toward endogenizing human capital, but both begin from Cobb–Douglas and Solow origins.

Lucas's approach is to assume that there is a tradeoff between using time to develop job skills and using time to produce output. Because time is divided between these two activities, a society can gain more output only at the expense of less education and training, and vice versa. C. I. Jones (2001) presents the following simplified version of the Lucas approach, using the Cobb–Douglas production function:

$$Y_t = K_t^\alpha (AH_t)^{1-\alpha}, \tag{5.2}$$

where $H_t = e^{\psi u} L_t$. Here, u represents the fraction of time that laborers spend acquiring new skills, so $1 - u$ is the fraction of time spent working in production activities. The labor force, L, is defined as $(1 - u)P$, where P is the total population, so this expression describes how the labor force shrinks as people take time off to obtain new skills.[1] The variable H is the level of human capital–adjusted labor, and the term ψ is the payoff for each additional unit increase in time spent obtaining skills. The level of technology is again represented by the index A; however, in this case, human capital augments labor, and technology augments human capital–adjusted labor.

The solution for the balanced growth path of output per worker in the Lucas model is

$$\frac{Y_t}{L_t} = \left(\frac{s}{n+g+\delta} \right)^{\frac{\alpha}{1-\alpha}} e^{\psi u} A_t. \tag{5.3}$$

The average level of human capital per worker, $e^{\psi u}$, is a constant. As a result, there is very little difference between this model and the traditional Solow model. A look back at equation (2.6) demonstrates how closely Lucas's human capital model follows the Solow model. The new parameters, ψ and u, become new standard variables, in that any permanent shock to either ψ or u will produce standard level effects in the model, and temporary shocks will produce transitory growth effects. The rate of output per worker still grows at the rate of technological progress, g, along a balanced growth path.

There are limits to how much of a shock to u is feasible given that laborers cannot spend more than 100 percent of their time developing skills. Society also gives up production with increases in the fraction u, so there are likely to be diminishing returns to developing skills. The 10th year of education may produce valuable training, but the 15th year probably less so, the 20th year even less, and so on.

If governments want to raise output per worker through increases in the amount of time spent obtaining job skills, they must consider what society gives up as more time and resources are devoted toward skills development. If time is better spent producing output than obtaining training, human capital returns might be so low as to make more investments in schooling counterproductive. In other words, investments in human capital should pass a benefit-cost test.

Policymakers may have more luck increasing ψ, the human capital payoff. Increasing ψ requires that knowledge improve over time such that the same amount of time devoted to training produces more human capital. More highly skilled teachers might accomplish this, as might more useful information in textbooks. The key is to improve the current state of knowledge or the mechanisms of transmitting knowledge to the young and unskilled.

Mankiw, Romer, and Weil (1992) take a slightly different approach in their model of human capital. Unlike in the Lucas model where human capital augments labor, these authors assume human capital is a separate input in the production function such that

$$Y_t = K_t^\alpha H_t^\beta (A_t L_t)^{1-\alpha-\beta}. \tag{5.4}$$

Note that the assumption of constant returns to scale is maintained, so α and β are between 0 and 1 and together sum to less than 1. Solving for the equation for output per worker along the balanced growth path yields

$$\frac{Y_t}{L_t} = \left[\left(\frac{s_K}{n+g+\delta} \right)^\alpha \left(\frac{s_H}{n+g+\delta} \right)^\beta \right]^{1-\alpha-\beta} A_t. \tag{5.5}$$

Here, s_K is the fraction of savings dedicated to physical capital accumulation, and s_H is the fraction of savings dedicated to human capital accumulation. Both forms of capital are assumed to depreciate at the same rate, δ. In this model, human capital is like physical capital in that it is generated by forgoing consumption—that is, saving more. Recall that in the Lucas model human capital results from forgoing production.

As in the Lucas model, permanent shocks to human capital produce level effects. Both models suggest that a more educated labor force will (with all else equal) be associated with a richer country, and this turns out to be the case empirically. Figure 5.1 plots the relationship between human capital levels in 2011, as measured by the Barro–Lee Educational Attainment Dataset (Feenstra, Inklaar, and Timmer 2013), and the level of output per worker across countries in the same year. There is a strong correlation between the two variables, with $R^2 = 0.30$, meaning human capital differences explain about one-third of the variation in output per worker across countries. There are some outliers in the model, such as Qatar, Brunei, and Luxembourg. Qatar's and Brunei's wealth are both largely explained by

Figure 5.1. Output per Worker and Human Capital, 2011

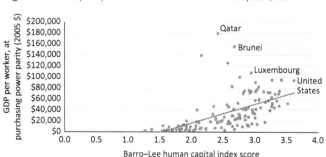

Source: Feenstra, Inklaar, and Timmer 2013.

natural resources such as oil, whereas Luxembourg is a very small country with an unusually large financial sector. Beyond such outliers, the relationship between human capital and the wealth of a nation is strong.

As with the Solow model, sustained, long-run growth in the Lucas and Mankiw–Romer–Weil models is determined exogenously by the rate of technological progress. However, these models can easily be modified so that positive spillover effects of human capital lead to endogenous growth, that is, long-run growth that is determined within the model itself as opposed to exogenously. Lucas (1988) presents a version of his model that includes such spillover effects, and the results look very similar to the AK model of economic growth and the learning-by-doing model to be discussed next. Nonetheless, when maintaining the assumption of a constant returns to scale production function and no spillovers, permanent shocks to human capital or its determinants produce level effects rather than growth rate effects.

AK MODELS

Until now, the models examined here have assumed that long-run growth is determined exogenously by the growth rate of technology. Now we turn to models where growth rates are generated endogenously—that is, within the model itself. Models of this type are known as *endogenous growth models*, and the simplest way to endogenize growth is to eliminate the assumption of diminishing returns to input factors in the production function. The most basic model to do this is the AK model, which assumes constant returns to capital.

The most well-known example of an AK model comes from Barro (1990). In his model, production is ruled by the function

$$y_t = f(k) = Ak_t, \qquad (5.6)$$

where A is a constant and y and k are the intensive forms of output and capital. Since A is a constant, its growth rate is 0, that is, $\dot{A}/A = g = 0$. As a result of this assumption, production still exhibits constant, and not increasing, returns to all inputs. In other words, if all inputs in production are doubled, aggregate production is still only doubled because the level of technology remains fixed. It is easy to show that the marginal product of capital, $f'(k) = A$, so that along a balanced growth path output per worker grows at the rate of consumption growth:

$$\frac{\dot{c}}{c} = \frac{1}{\theta}(A - \rho). \qquad (5.7)$$

Equation (5.7) is simply a restatement of equation (5.1) from the Ramsey–Cass–Koopmans model. Only now the interest rate is equal to A.

In the AK model, permanent increases in the savings rate have growth rate effects. This makes the AK model very similar to a precursor of the Solow model known as the *Harrod–Domar growth model*. Developed by Harrod (1939) and Domar (1946), that model explains growth as being largely driven by savings and capital formation. At a more granular level, the AK model implies that changes in the coefficient of relative risk aversion, θ, and in the rate of time preference, ρ, also have growth rate effects through their influence on savings behavior.

Limited empirical evidence supports the AK model because countries that save more do not always grow faster (Barro and Sala-i-Martin 2004; C. I. Jones 2001). Another problem is that there is no convergence in the AK model. The assumption of diminishing returns to capital is what causes convergence in the Solow model, so relaxing this assumption eliminates the tendency for countries to converge. This presents a problem for the AK model because in the real world there is significant evidence of convergence across countries, especially in the conditional sense.

Interestingly, there are also no transition dynamics in the AK model. Changes in the model take place instantly, so after experiencing a shock, the economy moves seamlessly to a new balanced growth path. In this sense, the world inside the AK model is always in the long run. Although these problems make the model somewhat unrealistic, the AK model becomes more plausible if capital is thought of broadly as encompassing human as well as physical capital (Barro and Sala-i-Martin 2004; Rebelo 1991). The model should probably be viewed even more broadly than this, however. AK models can be thought of as a general class of models that produce endogenous growth. As will be shown in the next section on learning-by-doing models, other models in the AK family also lead to endogenous growth without requiring this broad view of capital.

A central result of the AK model is that policies, including regulations, can produce growth rate effects. Any permanent change in savings behavior leads to changes in the growth rate of output per worker without any corresponding increase in technology. Encouraging prudent savings and investment or subsidizing job training and skills development produces hugely beneficial results in this model.

This result is interesting because growth that is driven by human capital and investment may not be as disruptive as technology-driven growth. Mandel (2004, xix) refers to this kind of capital-driven growth as "cautious growth" because it is less upsetting and disorderly than "exuberant growth" that is based on disruptive technological innovation. Thus, public policies that encourage investment may generate growth while also maintaining more support from the public.

The AK model is also consistent with empirical evidence that differing levels of capital do explain a fair amount of growth differences across countries. *Growth accounting* refers to the practice of disentangling the different determinants of growth. Those who have tried to quantify the contributions of capital, labor, and technology in a growth accounting framework do find a relationship between capital accumulation and growth rates. For example, capital formation is thought to explain about 30 percent of differences in cross-country growth rates (Caselli 2005). Solow model proponents might claim that these are only short-run growth differences and that in the long run only technology will still determine growth rates. Nonetheless, the long run takes a long time to arrive, and given the consistent relationship found between savings, capital formation, and growth, it seems that the basic insight of the AK and Harrod–Domar models—that capital formation matters for growth rates—is correct.

LEARNING-BY-DOING MODELS

Once economists drop the assumption of diminishing returns to capital, the door is opened to constant returns at the factor level and increasing returns to scale at the aggregate production level. Dropping the assumption of diminishing returns also allows inclusion of other interesting elements in a growth model, such as externalities. In economics, an externality refers to an attribute of a product that is unpriced in the market. This attribute affects third parties that are not participants in an economic exchange. The standard example is pollution, whereby buyers and sellers of a good (e.g., electricity) do not take into account the effect of their actions on others (e.g., breathers of polluted air). Therefore, the cost of the externality is not accounted for in the market price of the good (in this case, electricity).

In growth models, externalities are included by allowing changes in one variable to affect other variables. These can also be thought of as multiplier or spillover effects. One of the first models to include such spillover effects was the learning-by-doing model developed by Frankel (1962) and Arrow (1962). In the learning-by-doing model, the production process—rather than formal education—engenders learning, which leads to increases in productivity. This kind of informal learning process is a second form of knowledge-generating innovation that will be explored in the remaining chapters.

In the 1930s, engineers noticed that the labor hours required to produce a single airplane fell as the number of airplanes that were built increased. In other words, as aggregate output grew, there was a corresponding increase in productivity that could not be accounted for by the standard inputs of labor and capital. The learning-by-doing model was an attempt to explain this phenomenon by showing how worker productivity increases as a result of experience.

Learning by doing is similar to a phenomenon noticed by the 18th-century economist and political philosopher Adam Smith—that specialization tends to increase productivity. When workers divide production into different tasks and everyone specializes in a particular task, workers become more productive. This was the insight behind Henry Ford's famous moving assembly line for the production of his Model T cars.

In the learning-by-doing model, knowledge generation is a positive externality resulting from capital formation. Each firm faces the production function as shown in the following equation:

$$Y_{i,t} = a I_t K_{i,t}^{\alpha} L_{i,t}^{1-\alpha}, \tag{5.8}$$

where $Y_{i,t}$, $K_{i,t}$, and $L_{i,t}$ represent the firm-specific output, capital, and labor for each firm, i, at time t, and a is a constant level of technology that is distinct from the knowledge generated in the capital accumulation process. Each firm takes the average level of knowledge, I, as given in its production function. Here, $I_t = (K_t/L_t)^{\gamma}$, meaning knowledge is a function of the level of capital per worker.

There is no subscript i with the I term because I is a social variable that is given to everyone, as opposed to a variable that is unique to each firm. Each firm's investment in capital makes a small contribution to I, but no firm takes its individual contribution into account when deciding how much output to produce. In other words, I is a public good. It represents the stock of nonexcludable and nonrival public knowledge, which is an accidental byproduct of the production process. Once produced, knowledge is immediately and freely available to everyone.

Astute observers will notice that in the special case where $\gamma = 1 - \alpha$, the aggregate production function simplifies to

$$Y_t = aK_t, \tag{5.9}$$

which is the AK model again. The learning-by-doing model is therefore a special case of the AK model; as with the AK model, a permanent change in the savings rate produces growth rate effects. With respect to regulation, this implies that rules that reduce saving and investment lower growth rates and rules that increase saving and investment increase growth rates.

The learning-by-doing model might also be thought of as embodying a version of the 18th-century economist Adam Smith's invisible hand theorem. Smith noticed how individuals acting in their own self-interest can unintentionally bring about results that advance the public interest. Each firm in the learning-by-doing model, by acting to maximize its own profits, accidentally contributes to the public good through its contributions to the stock of public knowledge. This accidental byproduct of production increases the average level of knowledge in the economy, thereby increasing output per worker and wages unintentionally.

There is something very appealing about modeling economic growth as an accidental byproduct of human exchange. As described in chapter 6 on remaining puzzles in growth theory, there is still a great deal about growth that economists cannot explain. If growth is truly an unintended consequence of human interaction, this might be why, historically, identifying the causes of economic growth has been so difficult. Knowledge is also very difficult to measure. If tacit knowledge of the sort developed through learning and experience is a core determinant of growth, it is understandable that economists have a hard time pinning down the causes of growth.

The learning-by-doing model also corresponds nicely with many insights from the Austrian school of economics. Nobel laureate Friedrich A. Hayek (1984 [1968]) describes competition in the marketplace as a "discovery procedure," whereby firms discover new knowledge as they take part in the competitive market process. Knowledge, once uncovered, spreads throughout the economy by imitation and learning.

If growth really is largely an accidental byproduct of the production process, this poses problems for policymakers. Perhaps they might be able to stimulate the capital formation process through tax incentives or subsidies, but it is unlikely that they will be able to replicate the process by which new knowledge is uncovered. That takes competition, experimentation, and trial and error, which all together suggest a role for policy in fostering a competitive market, but probably not a role for micromanaging firm decisions. Removing barriers to competition, such as breaking up monopolies, would be a good idea under these circumstances. Removing regulations that limit entry into an industry is another way to enhance competition.

There may be another role for policy as well. An interesting implication of the learning-by-doing model is that a decentralized free market economy does not produce a Pareto efficient outcome. Pareto efficiency refers to a situation whereby no one can be made better off without making another person worse off. The learning-by-doing model deviates from Pareto efficiency because the private marginal product of capital for each firm and the social marginal product of capital diverge. Thus, each firm underinvests in capital, and I remains below its socially optimal level. Even if firms could come together to agree to each invest in the optimal amount of capital each period, there is a strong incentive for firms to shirk from the agreement because there is an incentive to get a free ride off the investment efforts of others.

The growth rate of the economy will be below its optimal level for these reasons. Under laissez-faire, there is too little investment in the economy relative to an ideal state, so either investment could be subsidized (directly or through tax credits) or policymakers could impose a tax of some kind (preferably the lump sum form to avoid distortions) on consumption. The key question will be at what level to impose the tax or subsidy. This information may be unknowable. Furthermore, government already taxes and subsidizes countless forms of investment to varying degrees, so it is difficult to know whether there is too much or too little investment at any given time. Finally, most taxes are not implemented in a lump sum manner. Thus, taxation efforts to bring social and private marginal costs into alignment will produce economic distortions in their own right that must be weighed against any social benefits that result from improving market efficiency in other ways.

Although not discussed in detail here, the constant returns to scale models examined thus far assume perfect competition. This assumption means that prices of outputs equal the marginal costs of those outputs, and that factor inputs are paid their marginal products. Because the externality in the learning-by-doing model is completely nonexcludable—that is, firms are unable to exclusively use the knowledge they generate—perfect competition can still be assumed in this model. As shown in the next section of this chapter, however, when firms are able to internalize some fraction of the knowledge they produce (i.e., they are able to find ways to exclude other firms from using the knowledge), the assumption of perfect competition is no longer tenable.

MODELS THAT ENDOGENIZE TECHNOLOGICAL CHANGE

The first generation of endogenous growth models used the capital formation process to explain growth in the economy. Examples include the Harrod–Domar model, the learning-by-doing model, and the AK model. Not surprisingly, some scholars also sought ways to endogenize the mysterious technological change variable in growth models. These economists sought to model technological advances in society, including the process of generating new knowledge. Unlike the learning-by-doing model where knowledge creation is an accidental byproduct of production, in this new generation of growth models, scholars would explain knowledge creation as a purposeful activity on the part of firms. The most famous model to do this is the model of Paul M. Romer (1990), whose work led to a revival of growth theory that came to be known as *new growth theory*.

Romer's growth model contains two sectors, an approach that can be traced back to Uzawa (1964). One sector of the economy produces final goods intended for consumers, whereas a second sector—the research and development (R&D) sector—invents new durable capital goods that are used as inputs in the final goods–producing sector. These durable capital goods might be thought of as new ideas, new designs, or new templates that expand society's ability to produce final goods for consumers.

In other words, innovation in Romer's model shows up as a wider variety of goods in the marketplace.

In the model, some fraction a_L of the labor force is employed in the R&D sector—these people might be thought of as researchers—while the fraction $1 - a_L$ of the labor force is employed in the production of final goods for consumers. The technology index A represents the number of ideas, templates, or designs produced by the R&D sector, which has a production function such as

$$\dot{A}_t = \tau [a_L L_t]^\lambda A_t^\phi, \tag{5.10}$$

where τ is a measure of the productivity of researchers, and the parameter λ explains how adding new researchers affects the rate of change in new idea creation. For example, if $\lambda > 1$, there are increasing returns to adding new researchers, so each new researcher makes all existing researchers more productive.

The number of researchers has increased considerably in recent decades, as has the total amount spent on R&D in developed countries, so empirical evidence suggests that there are not increasing returns to adding researchers (C. I. Jones 1995). Otherwise, increases in growth rates would have been seen across the developed world. The parameter λ is more likely to lie below 1 for this reason and may even be negative in cases where the marginal researcher actually undermines the pursuit of knowledge rather than advances it.

Increasing the fraction of the labor force engaged in R&D has a two-pronged effect in the Romer model. First, output immediately falls as workers shift from producing final goods to conducting research. This first effect means there is an immediate drop in output per worker. Next, the growth rate of technology immediately rises as more research is conducted. This second effect produces a positive growth rate effect.[2]

The parameter Ø is likely positive. It represents how the existing stock of ideas affects the difficulty of discovering new ones. If researchers are "standing on the shoulders of giants," to borrow a phrase from Isaac Newton, then future discoveries build on previous discoveries, and Ø is greater than 0. For example, the development of the lightbulb built on the discovery of electricity. However, if past discoveries make future discoveries harder, Ø is less than 1. This might be the case if all the technological low-hanging fruit has been picked and further innovations require greater and greater investments (Cowen 2011).

As in the Solow model, output per worker grows at the same rate as A. However, in the Romer model the growth rate of technology is not always a constant along a balanced growth path. In fact, the growth rate *of the growth rate* of technology is described by the function

$$\frac{\dot{g}_{A_t}}{g_{A_t}} = \lambda n + (\phi - 1)g_{A_t}, \qquad (5.11)$$

where the growth rate of g_A at time t depends on two factors: (a) the labor force growth rate (weighted on the basis of the returns to adding new researchers) and (b) the growth rate of technology at time t (weighted by whether having a higher level of technology makes new ideas easier or more difficult to uncover). This tendency for the growth rate to change along a balanced growth path is a major departure from the models discussed heretofore in this book.

A core reason for this difference is because for any value of Ø greater than 1, the growth rate of the economy will be increasing over time. Romer developed his model in part because he thought growth rates were increasing over time, and he was seeking a way to explain this phenomenon (P. M. Romer 1986). Looking back through history—centuries as opposed to years or decades—there is evidence that the growth rate of the developed world may be gradually increasing. This largely follows from the fact that growth was stagnant throughout most of human history.

However, C. I. Jones (1999) points out that any value of Ø equal to or greater than 1 produces counterintuitive results with respect to population growth because just increasing the *level* of the labor force results in a growth rate effect. Changes in the growth rate of the labor force result in exponential increases in growth rates. Such a finding is sometimes referred to as a *scale effect* in the literature. A scale effect occurs when there are increasing returns to scale in certain variables in a growth model. Recall that the AK model reviewed earlier assumed constant returns to capital and not increasing returns.

Population scale effects are unlikely to hold in the real world because these kinds of returns are just not seen in the empirical data. For this reason, Ø probably lies below 1, which means that the growth rate of output per worker is determined largely by the growth rate (and not the level) of the labor force, n.

In the more realistic case where Ø < 1, changes in the growth *rate* of the labor force produce growth rate effects, and changes in the *level* of the labor force result in level effects. And because growth is primarily determined by the labor force growth rate in the model, and this variable is itself an exogenous variable, models such as this have come to be known as *semiendogenous* growth models. Technological change has been endogenized in the model, but the growth rate along a balanced growth path is still determined by forces outside the model. Creative destruction and quality ladder models, which are discussed next, are also classes of semiendogenous growth models.

There is another interesting property of the Romer model. When $\emptyset < 1$, growth in per capita income is a stationary, mean-reverting process. This just means that growth rates tend to be fairly constant over time, which is consistent with the empirical data (at least over the past century or two). But if $\emptyset$ lies below but very close to 1, the economy will behave *almost as if* $\emptyset = 1$ for long stretches of time. That is, the closer $\emptyset$ is to 1, the longer will be the transition to a new balanced growth path. As a result, short-run changes in growth rates as part of the transition dynamics from a level effect could last for very extended periods of time, perhaps even decades. Thus, the distinction between level effects and growth rate effects may be hard to decipher in the real world (Cochrane 2015). This could explain why factors such as saving and capital accumulation appear to influence growth rates in growth accounting exercises, even though models such as the Solow model suggest there should be no long-run effect.

The Romer model is unique from the previously reviewed models in another important way. The nature of knowledge in the Romer model is very different from the pure public-good form of knowledge seen in the learning-by-doing model. This is perhaps the most important contribution of P. M. Romer (1990). In his model, as in the real world, firms deliberately invest in new technologies, so there must be some financial incentive for firms to do so. Recall that in the learning-by-doing model, new knowledge is a public good that is instantly available to all other firms. It had to be accidental for the model to explain why firms would create new knowledge at all.

The fact that firms do invest in R&D in the real world suggests at least some fraction of new knowledge is not a pure public good. Otherwise, every other firm would get a free ride off the knowledge-creation efforts of others, and there would be no incentive to invest in R&D. Firms must be able to keep some new discoveries to themselves—at least for a period of time—and this provides sufficient incentive to partially overcome the problem of free riders. The excludable component of knowledge might be the result of secrecy, or it could follow from deliberate policy interventions, such as patent protections.

That some knowledge is excludable undermines a fundamental assumption of the models examined thus far—the assumption of perfect competition. If firms are engaging in large up-front R&D expenditures to generate discoveries, pricing cannot possibly equal marginal cost. The first unit of production will be very expensive when large R&D investments are required to produce it, but costs will fall dramatically with each additional unit produced. Consider the case of a pharmaceutical where the first pill costs a billion dollars to produce but the second pill costs just a penny. If all firms set prices equal to marginal cost, any firm that engages in R&D will quickly go out of business in this kind of market.

Many growth theorists have thus switched to models of monopolistic competition of the sort developed by Chamberlin (1933) and Dixit and Stiglitz (1977), and this switch in turn implies that there are two kinds of distortions in the economy, that is, deviations from Pareto efficiency. First, if firms set prices above marginal cost (which must be true to explain how firms that engage in R&D stay in business), then these firms must have some monopoly power. When a firm has monopoly power, this means it will restrict output to maximize profits, and aggregate output lies below the socially optimal level. Second, too little output also implies too little demand for inputs, such as R&D, and because R&D drives growth in the Romer model, growth rates will be below the socially optimal level.

These findings suggest several possible roles for government. First, there may be a role in designing intellectual property protections. Without adequate protections, firms may lack the incentive to invest enough in new technologies because they cannot internalize the benefits of these new technologies. The more nonexcludable an invention is, the more likely that there is a role for such protections to play. But there is a tradeoff to consider between incentivizing investment and the losses to society from monopoly restrictions on output. Furthermore, recall that patent protections can also result in a tragedy of the anticommons if patents are overissued.

There may also be a role for government in subsidizing R&D. If firms are underinvesting in R&D, the government could encourage it directly through subsidies or indirectly through tax credits. Subsidies to final-goods producers would accomplish the same end by increasing demand for R&D inputs. However, before the government rushes in and begins subsidizing R&D, there are several factors to consider. When subsidies are financed by any means other than lump sum taxes, the taxes will create distortions that must be weighed against the benefits of the subsidies. Second, investment in R&D must actually be productive. Historically, governments have not had a better track record than the private sector at picking investment projects (OECD 2003). This suggests that R&D tax credits that give private firms control over the selection of projects may be more effective than having government invest directly in new research.

Aside from the scale effects that can arise in the Romer model, the model also has some other unrealistic features. Countries that remain mired in poverty often have high population growth rates, whereas many rich countries have low or stagnant population growth rates. Population growth does not appear to be a sufficient condition for economic growth. At the global level, population growth and economic growth move more closely together (Barro and Sala-i-Martin 2004; Kremer 1993b), but this may be because higher incomes allow more people to be sustained on Earth, rather than the other way around (that is, a bigger population causes higher incomes). Or, it may be that human capital–adjusted population growth is what really matters.

A final lesson from the Romer model relates to free trade. There are clearly benefits from engaging with greater numbers of people. Expanding the network of people that firms interact with means expanding the network of ideas. A larger market also implies greater demand for new ideas, which incentivizes idea creation. Adam Smith suggested in his book *The Wealth of Nations* that incomes in countries are dependent on the size of the market. A larger market allows for more specialization not just in physical production but in idea production as well.

CREATIVE DESTRUCTION AND QUALITY LADDER MODELS

In the Romer model, innovation shows up as changes in the number of products available. Economists have developed other classes of models to account for innovation in the form of quality improvements that occur over time. The most important contributions in this literature are from Grossman and Helpman (1991), who developed a theory of "quality ladders" in economic growth, and Aghion and Howitt (1992), whose "creative destruction" model of growth explains obsolescence (i.e., the process of new products replacing old ones over time).

Quality ladder models treat products as if they are on a race up a ladder. Each time an entrepreneur develops an improvement, the product moves up one rung on the ladder. Creative destruction models, named after the term coined by Austrian-born economist Joseph Schumpeter (1942), explain how old products become obsolete and disappear from the market over time as new and better products are developed.

As in the Romer model, firms have some monopoly power in both the quality ladder and creative destruction models. Several externalities are also present. First, when an innovation occurs, consumers pay the same price for a better product. The result is a spillover benefit to consumers as products move up each rung of the quality ladder. Second, producer profits decline for rivals when a firm innovates and takes the business of its competitors. This externality is known as *business stealing*, and it creates a misalignment of incentives because the benefits of innovation are permanent for consumers but only temporary for producers.

At first glance, business stealing looks like only a pecuniary externality—that is, an externality resulting from a price change that is a pure transfer from one party to another—but in fact other spillover effects arise. If businesses are not fully compensated when other innovations build on the quality improvements they developed, firms will be discouraged from investing in an optimal level of R&D.

Here is how this can happen. Consider Isaac Newton and Gottfried Wilhelm Leibniz, who are both credited with having developed calculus. Neither of these individuals was compensated during their lifetimes for the millions of ways in which calculus is put to use today. In an ideal world, these individuals would have been compensated, because so many aspects of modern life would not be possible without these innovations from the past. Without a compensation scheme for past inventors, one can expect there to be too little innovation. Even worse, competition will reduce the expected duration of monopoly rents accrued from innovation—so the more firms that are competing, the more inventors who will be discouraged from inventing and the more firms that will be discouraged from spending on R&D.

Interestingly, there can also be too much R&D in creative destruction and quality ladder models. Much like there is social waste when firms compete for transfers from the government (an activity known as *rent-seeking*), there can also be social waste if competition drives firms to overinvest in R&D as they seek to capture the monopoly profits of their rivals.

Creative destruction and quality ladder models again demonstrate the importance of finding the right balance between intellectual property protections and monopoly power. Too little intellectual property protection could mean that firms will not invest in R&D enough, whereas too much protection could encourage wasteful competition for transfers. One solution that has been proposed is to force innovators to compensate their immediate predecessors (Barro and Sala-i-Martin 2004). However, quality improvements are notoriously difficult to measure, and even if they could be measured perfectly, it is hard to know which ideas formed the basis for succeeding innovations.

A predecessor payment scheme is likely to prove impossible to implement. Unfortunately, these problems have no simple solutions.

TECHNOLOGY TRANSFER

In the economic growth models explored here thus far, innovation is driven by the creation of new knowledge, new products, and new quality improvements. Such innovation arises from formal education and training, on-the-job experience, and R&D investments. However, firms and individuals also have the ability to imitate innovations created by others. When businesses are not operating along the *technological frontier* (i.e., using the latest and best technology), they have the option of either creating new innovations themselves or imitating the innovative practices of others. The process of transferring technological knowledge through imitation is known as *technology transfer*.

Usually, technology transfer models speak in terms of countries. For example, middle- and lower-middle-income countries such as China and India may be able to grow quickly by simply adopting the practices and technologies generated elsewhere, such as Western Europe and the United States. The same phenomenon applies to firms. Firms can be divided into *leading firms* that operate along the technological frontier and *follower firms* that lag. Firms operating at the technological frontier have no choice but to innovate by creating new knowledge if they want to grow. But follower firms have the option of imitating the technologies developed in leading firms if they do not want to be innovators themselves. And just as there are costs associated with innovating, so too there are costs associated with imitating—although in general, imitating should prove easier than innovating. The costs of imitation include the time and effort it takes to copy a product design, to adjust a product to fit the preferences of different consumers, and to adopt the modes of production from one industry and apply them to new industries.

There are also likely to be diminishing returns to imitation. Some innovations are very easy to copy. On one hand, it might be easy to imitate a dating website and create a similar website targeted to a new demographic. On the other hand, supply chain management techniques in factories might be much harder to copy and may not have the same payoffs in other industries if workers respond differently in different environments. In other words, some technologies have limited applicability outside a single narrow use, or they may simply be too costly to copy because of their complexity.

Just as diminishing returns to capital create convergence among economies in the Solow model, diminishing returns to technology transfer create convergence tendencies. The further a country or firm is from the technological frontier, the faster that country or firm will grow. This type of growth might be dubbed *technological catch-up growth*, to be distinguished from the traditional *capital-based* catch-up growth found in the Solow model. In essence, imitation is another way to increase g in the Solow model. The rate of growth will be fast in firms and countries that begin from a low level of technology, just as it is fast in firms and countries that begin from a low level of capital per worker.

Human capital also plays a role in technology transfer. Some technologies are relatively easy to learn, such as operating a soft-serve ice cream machine. Other technologies take years of schooling to master, such as computer programming or statistical analysis. So human capital operates through another channel that facilitates growth. Raising the skill level of workers speeds up the process by which technology is transferred from leading to follower firms and countries.

Because knowledge has attributes of a pure public good, technologies invented in one place can have spillover effects in other places, as in the learning-by-doing model. At the country level, technological advances in high-income countries act like a form of foreign aid to lower-income countries. Cell phones are an obvious example of a technology that has raised living standards for some of the poorest individuals in the world. Such a result was probably not the intention of those who created cell phones, but it is nonetheless a social benefit that should be recognized.

If policymakers in rich countries think they have a duty to assist individuals in poor countries—and many people would agree they do—one of the best ways they can accomplish this goal is to spur innovation at home. For regulators, this means that the costs of blocking new innovations and the benefits of encouraging new innovations extend beyond a country's borders. Considering that it is poor people in less well-off countries who stand to gain the most from technological advances, this benefit provides a strong argument for allowing socially beneficial innovations to arrive as quickly as possible.

Policymakers should also seek to extend intellectual property rights abroad through treaties or to find ways to encourage more foreign direct investment at home and abroad. When property rights are protected, firms will find it easier to protect their innovations abroad. Firms might also protect their investments by purchasing the foreign firms that adopt their inventions, which is a reason not to be afraid when foreign firms buy up domestic ones. Not only does this process help secure property rights around the world, it speeds up the process of technology diffusion. Workers can learn from technological leaders by working directly for them.

Regulatory complexity also can discourage technology transfer. If a country's regulatory code is too complex, this creates a hurdle to investing. Investors are already more likely to invest in their own countries because of a home bias effect. If they do not understand a foreign country's legal code or think it will be arbitrarily enforced, investment will be discouraged.

Some follower countries or firms may see a short-term benefit from using the inventions of others without compensating them. In the long run, however, this practice is likely to discourage foreign direct investment, slow technology transfer, and lead to reciprocal stealing when the followers eventually become leaders themselves in areas.

CHANGES IN THE ELASTICITY OF SUBSTITUTION

The production function that forms the foundation for the economic growth models discussed in this book is the famous Cobb–Douglas production function. One of the useful features of this function, indeed one of the main reasons Cobb and Douglas (1928) first conceived of it, is its assumption of unit elasticity of substitution between capital and labor.

The elasticity of substitution describes the change in relative demand for capital and labor when there is a change in the relative cost of these inputs. Unit elasticity means that for every 1 percent rise in the ratio of prices between labor and capital, w/r, where w represents the wage rate for labor and r is the rental rate on capital, there is a corresponding 1 percent rise in the ratio of aggregate capital to labor demanded in the economy, K/L. Unit elasticity of substitution between capital and labor is a convenient assumption because it simplifies the math in the model, but it is not likely to be true most of the time in the real world.

In the early 1960s, a new class of production functions was developed to relax the unit elasticity assumption (Arrow et al. 1961). Production functions of this class are known as *constant elasticity of substitution production functions*, and an example of such a function is

$$Y_t = A_t [\alpha K_t^\vartheta + (1-\alpha)L_t^\vartheta]^{\frac{1}{\vartheta}}, \qquad (5.12)$$

where $\vartheta < 1$ and the elasticity of substitution between capital and labor is defined as $\sigma = 1/(1 - \vartheta)$. The parameter α is a share parameter between 0 and 1. In the special case where $\vartheta = 0$, equation (5.12) becomes the Cobb–Douglas production function, where $\sigma = 1$. This result can be shown by taking the limit of equation (5.12) as $\vartheta \to 0$. Similarly, as $\vartheta \to -\infty$, the production function approaches the fixed proportions production function made famous by Leontief (1941).

An interesting result to emerge from constant elasticity of substitution production functions is that growth models based on these functions produce endogenous growth when ϑ lies between 0 and 1. In such cases, there is high substitutability between capital and labor (i.e., σ is greater than 1). When this happens, the property of diminishing returns to capital per worker gradually vanishes as capital per worker asymptotically approaches infinity (Barro and Sala-i-Martin 2004). With a high-enough savings rate, changes in the savings rate produce growth rate effects rather than level effects, but this property of the model also violates fundamental assumptions of most growth models, known as the *Inada conditions* (Inada 1963). These conditions state that as $k \to 0$, $f'(k) \to \infty$, and that as $k \to \infty$, $f'(k) \to 0$. In other words, this assumption states that the marginal product of capital per worker diminishes as capital per worker grows, and the marginal product of capital per worker grows as capital per worker shrinks.

When ϑ lies between 0 and 1, meaning there is a high elasticity of substitution, $f'(k)$ approaches a positive constant as $k \to \infty$. Recent empirical estimates suggest that σ is likely to be less than 1 (Chirinko 2008), so the Inada conditions likely hold in the real world, which is also consistent with conventional wisdom. But there are reasons to believe these conditions may be fragile. For example, the theory of wealth inequality proposed by Piketty (2014) depends on an elasticity of substitution that is greater than 1 (Rognlie 2015). Piketty argues that wealth inequality increases in an economy where $r > g$, a condition known as the *transversality condition*. That $r > g$ is a standard assumption in growth models and is believed to be true in the real world, at least in healthy economies (Abel et al. 1989). Piketty seems to believe that wealth inequality is a natural outgrowth of a capitalist economy, but another possibility is that wealth inequality is an outgrowth of an economy with high substitutability between capital and labor.

Many forces might bring about this situation. Technology can make it easier to substitute capital and labor. For example, supermarket cashiers can be replaced by self-service cash registers, and tollbooth operators can be replaced by E-ZPass lanes. This creates an interesting bridge between the *wealth* inequality theory of Piketty and the *income* inequality theory of Cowen (2013). Cowen's story of inequality is based on the idea that individuals with job skills that are complementary to new technologies are likely to earn high incomes in the future, whereas individuals whose skills are replaceable by new technologies will earn lower incomes. It may be that inequality is not so much a natural outcome of a capitalist economy as it is a natural outgrowth of technological innovation.

Regulators may not have much control over the long-run progress of technology, but they can certainly influence the ability of firms to substitute capital and labor. For example, they can make it more difficult to fire workers by empowering labor unions. However, such protections could backfire if firms are discouraged from hiring workers in the first place because of high labor costs.

Regulators clearly influence the relative prices that affect aggregate demand for capital and labor as well. Everything from workplace safety regulations to rules mandating that employers provide such benefits as paid parental leave or health insurance will influence the price of labor and encourage capital substitution. Raising the minimum hourly wage is also likely to encourage automatizing human labor. Of course, capital is taxed and regulated to varying degrees as well, which encourages substitution toward labor. Which production input is given preferable treatment in the aggregate is unclear, although in recent decades the share of national income going to labor has declined and the share going to capital has risen.

A key question is whether the elasticity of substitution is indeed rising over time. Rognlie (2015) makes the important point that it is *net* elasticity of substitution—that is, the elasticity of substitution *after depreciation* is taken into account—that matters for inequality purposes. Unfortunately, most estimates in the literature are estimates of gross elasticity. Rognlie assumes that net elasticity must be lower than gross elasticity, but his argument hinges on the assumption that capital depreciates whereas labor does not.

When labor is augmented by human capital, it is not clear whether the assumption that labor does not depreciate is realistic. For instance, extended periods of unemployment can lead to the erosion of worker skills. Technology also erodes worker skills. For example, those who know how to repair typewriters will probably have trouble finding employment with this skill today.

Some human capital models of growth even include a depreciation factor. The model of Mankiw, Romer, and Weil (1992) assumes that human capital and physical capital depreciate at the same rate. If technology is causing labor to depreciate faster—that is, job skills are eroding more quickly over time because of technological advances—the net elasticity of substitution could actually be *above* the empirical estimates of gross elasticity found in the literature. If the net elasticity of substitution is high enough, the Inada conditions could be violated, and wealth inequality could rise.

Whether this situation has been true in the past, is true now, or will be true in the future is unclear. However, the possibility of this scenario poses another challenge for public policy because of the chance of an interaction effect between regulation and technology. If technology is raising the elasticity of substitution and regulation has a tendency to favor capital over labor, regulations could be contributing to wealth inequality through the mechanisms described here.

6
The Roles of Institutions and Population

Despite significant advancements in the theory and empirics of economic growth, many mysteries remain. Macroeconomics is a notoriously difficult discipline because it seeks to explain so much complexity with so few variables and relatively few data. The process of uncovering the sources of growth has largely been about experimenting with different variables that for theoretical reasons seem important. Over time economists have been able to weed out the variables that appear to be less important and identify those with more explanatory power.

To see how far economic growth theory has come, consider that more than 50 years ago the economist Nicholas Kaldor (1961, 178) highlighted six "stylized facts" about economic growth. Stylized facts are accepted empirical observations that researchers seek to explain. Kaldor's six facts focus on the contribution of capital accumulation to economic growth. When Kaldor wrote his paper, savings and capital accumulation were thought to be the most important contributors to growth. Economists since then have learned that these factors can explain only a fraction of the growth differentials observed across countries.

In 2010, economists C. I. Jones and P. M. Romer (2010) updated Kaldor's list, highlighting the new stylized facts that require explaining by the next generation of growth economists. Their facts relate to ideas, institutions, population, and human capital. Economists are now in general agreement that these four factors matter for economic growth, but the micro-level mechanisms by which these factors influence macro-level growth remain poorly understood. Furthermore, it is not clear if these inputs themselves are what fundamentally drives growth or whether these variables are correlated with or caused by something more fundamental.

In recent decades, much attention in the economic growth and development literature has focused on the role of institutions. When economists talk about institutions, they are referring to the rules that constrain human economic and social behavior. The late Nobel laureate Douglass North (1991, 98), whose major contribution was to make institutions more central to economic theory, defined institutions as "rules of the game." Rules bind human behavior and shape the incentives people face in their economic lives. Some rules are formal, such as laws written by legislatures or regulations written by regulatory agencies. Other rules are informal, such as social and cultural norms that pressure us to be kind to our neighbors or to tell the truth. Institutions are extremely important for economic development—so important that some prominent economists call institutions a "fundamental cause of long-run growth" (Acemoglu, Johnson, and Robinson 2005).

Because institutions are so important, economists sometimes add an index of social infrastructure to the production functions in their models to estimate the contributions of institutions to economic growth. Such indices attempt to measure things such as the strength of property rights in a country, the rule of law, credible contract arrangements, the level of corruption, social levels of trust, or the degree of rent-seeking in society.[1] It turns out that social levels of trust can explain some differences in growth rates across countries (Zak and Knack 2001). Trust is also negatively correlated with regulation (Aghion et al. 2010).

Several difficulties arise when using indices of social infrastructure. First, the quality of institutions is very difficult to measure, so economists must be creative when they attempt to do so. Second, social infrastructure tends to be correlated with other factors, such as culture or religion. Max Weber (1930 [1904]), the German sociologist, thought the wealth of nations was driven in part by protestant values. As another example, an economist regressing output per worker on an index of social infrastructure in Switzerland might find a strong correlation between institutions and growth. But the fundamental cause of economic growth might simply be the Swiss culture that produces both strong institutions and steady growth. Most likely, there is a feedback loop between culture and institutions whereby culture shapes institutions and institutions shape culture (Alesina and Giuliano 2015).

There is a similar debate about the role that geography plays in economic growth. It turns out that latitude is highly correlated with GDP per capita (Bloom and Sachs 1998). For hundreds of years, observers have noticed that countries near the equator tend to be less developed than countries farther from the equator.[2] Jared Diamond (1997) is one of the best-known scholars to argue for the importance of geography in economic development. He contends that geographical happenstance determined mightily which groups were able to adopt certain technologies, develop agriculture, or generate immunities from diseases. See figure 6.1.

Acemoglu, Johnson, and Robinson (2001) think that colonialism explains the link between institutions and

Figure 6.1. GDP per Capita and Latitude, 2014

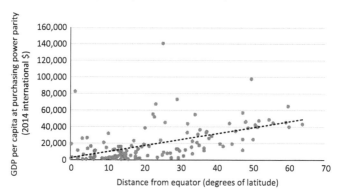

Sources: Hall and Jones 1999; World Bank Development Indicators.

geography. They argue that during the colonial period Europeans set up more *inclusive* institutions in places that had lower disease rates and a more hospitable environment for settlement. Alternatively, in those places that were less hospitable for economic development, such as parts of South America, Europeans created *extractive* institutions to expropriate wealth from those regions— regions where they never planned to settle permanently. These inclusive and extractive institutions persisted long after colonists left, either facilitating long-run growth or entrenching a culture of rent-seeking and corruption.

The debate about institutions and geography is far from settled. Some economists, such as Rodrik, Subramanian, and Trebbi (2004), argue that the effects of geography are weak and that they still operate primarily through institutional quality. Other economists, such as Sachs (2003), point to examples where geography has had direct effects on income per capita without any link to institutions. For example, many debilitating diseases, such as malaria, are far more common in areas near the equator. Distance from a coast also matters. Indeed, Adam Smith noted that cities with access to water tended to have higher living standards, which he attributed to access to global markets.

In all likelihood, geography does have direct effects on growth while also contributing to growth through institutions. But even more fundamental forces could be driving institutions. Comin, Easterly, and Gong (2010) point out that countries' practices of technology adoption from as far back as 1000 BC are strongly correlated with income per capita and technology adoption practices today. Using migration data to control for the historical places of origin of modern populations, these authors find that certain peoples, for cultural, historical, or perhaps genetic reasons, have been more open to adopting new technologies. For whatever reason, these tendencies seem to have persisted for hundreds, even thousands, of years.

This observation suggests that something much deeper may be going on than just cultural forces. Spolaore and Wacziarg (2013) point to some of the transmission mechanisms by which our ancestors might have passed on traits that support economic development, some of which are biological. G. Jones (2012) shows how cognitive skill is associated with technology diffusion, which comports with the idea that human capital and technology transfer are closely related. Perhaps intelligence even influenced human migration patterns thousands of years ago, leading to a connection between intelligence and geography. In fact, time preference and geography appear to be linked (Galor and Özak 2014). Furthermore, patience contributes to savings and capital formation, and high-intelligence

Figure 6.2. GDP per Capita and Child Mortality, 2014

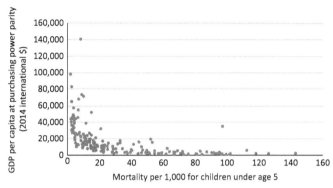

Source: World Bank Development Indicators.

people tend to be more patient (G. Jones 2015). At some point, economists may need to endogenize the parameters ρ and θ for underlying genetic characteristics.

Another possibility is that better nutrition improves cognitive skills, which facilitates human capital development and, by extension, spurs growth. Better health is strongly associated with higher income (Smith 1999), and negative health outcomes, such as child mortality, tend to fall with higher income. This is demonstrated in figure 6.2. Perhaps one reason humans lived in grinding poverty for so many thousands of years was simply because they were not healthy enough to build human capital. With adequate nourishment came opportunities to invent, to develop skills, and to build social infrastructure. This history suggests that health, geography, culture, cognitive skill, institutions, patience, ideas, and growth are all linked.

Unfortunately, the lessons for regulators here are far from clear. Respecting private property rights, enforcing contracts, and resisting the temptation to expropriate wealth all facilitate good institutions and improve growth.

It certainly cannot hurt for policymakers to aspire to these goals. But it is also not clear that in those places that lack good institutions the solution is simply to plant new institutions in place of old ones. Underlying forces, like the roots of a weed, may prevent healthy institutions from arising in the first place. Simply pulling the weed from the dirt will not change the underlying fundamentals that caused the weed to grow in the first place.

A better option is for regulators to embrace a culture that respects new technologies. Whatever the underlying causes, cultures that are more open to new technologies tend to thrive. Regulators should resist the demands of interest groups that are displaced by new technologies and should work to explain to the public the benefits of new technologies, even when those benefits also carry risks. Regulators who encourage safe experimentation with new technologies will promote growth more than those who act as gatekeepers to technological change.

THE ROLE OF POPULATION

As far back as the late 18th century (Malthus 1798), debate has raged among economists about whether a growing population raises living standards or promotes poverty. The Solow model takes the extreme position that faster population growth lowers the level of output per person, whereas other models, such as the Romer model, go to the opposite extreme.

The truth probably lies between these two positions, but where along the continuum the world lies is unclear. Empirically, the relationship between population and growth is vague. Many countries with fast population growth have historically grown slowly, whereas places with slow population growth often grow quickly. Only at the global level is the relationship between population and output per worker fairly reliable; even this relationship might be misleading if the correlation exists because it is rising income that allows more people to inhabit the earth.

A bias permeates the literature on the economics of ideas as well, which is that only good ideas result from having more people. But of course, people come up with bad ideas all the time. Sometimes bad ideas can take civilization down wrong turns, thereby leading to terrible destruction and misery. Communism is a particularly salient example of a bad idea that has destroyed millions of lives and that has taken several generations to recover from.

Sometimes the problem is not whether there are too many or too few people but instead whether a fixed number of people are allocated optimally across professions. Many people are not able to be as productive as they could be because they cannot, for one reason or another, enter the profession where they would be most productive. One reason for this might be discrimination (Hsieh et al. 2013). Policies that limit the free movement of people can also lead to a suboptimal allocation of people in the labor force. In cases where freedom of movement is necessarily limited, such as internationally, public policies that promote trade might improve the allocation of resources without requiring people to move.

Micro-level misallocations of these kinds can actually lower total factor productivity at the macro-level, thereby lowering growth rates (C. I. Jones 2013). The channels by which micro-misallocations lead to macroeconomic inefficiencies remain poorly understood, but some kind of spillover effect is an obvious possible explanation. The best option for policymakers is to, wherever possible, allow free movement of people, discourage discriminatory practices, and encourage trade across regions where movement is necessarily limited.

7

Conclusion

Many economists would love to claim that all a society needs to spur faster economic growth is more investment in R&D and more immigration. Indeed, some economists do make such proclamations. But nothing is so simple when it comes to economic growth. Most likely there are diminishing returns to many inputs in production, including labor, R&D, capital, and human capital. As a result, it is very hard to increase growth rates sustainably over the long term. And that may be a core reason why very long-run growth rates have held remarkably constant in higher-income countries over the past century and a half.

Nonetheless, there are some takeaways from the growth models surveyed in this book. The first lesson is twofold: (a) innovation matters and (b) a culture that embraces innovation should be promoted to a great extent. This book identifies a number of sources of innovation, including formal education and job training, informal tacit learning through experience and specialization, new products, quality improvements, and knowledge transfer through imitation. Regulators should seek to nurture and promote these sources of innovation, to avoid encouraging fear of new technology, and to support a culture of progress through technological change.

Another lesson of this book is that the cumulative effect of all policies is likely to matter most for economic growth. A single policy by itself probably will not have growth rate effects unless it encourages or discourages the adoption of a general purpose technology. Together, however, all policies can interact in ways that cause growth rate effects. This fact is particularly important because the regulatory code in the United States has consistently grown over time. As figure 7.1 demonstrates, federal regulation in this country has been growing, in terms of both the number of pages in the *Code of Federal Regulations* and the number of regulatory restrictions contained in the code. This means the regulatory system has become more complex over time, which in turn implies that significant unintended consequences of policy are more likely to occur. Going forward, policymakers need to address the important problem of how to control the growth of regulation.

Regulators must also approach potential GPTs with great care. They should seek to create a climate whereby discovery of new GPTs is more likely to occur and where the development and diffusion of potential GPTs is not stifled. Nanotechnology and biotechnology are two possibilities for what the next GPTs might be. Although GPTs can also create disruptions to particular subsets of the population, the long-run benefits generally vastly outweigh the costs, and the benefits should be explained to the public in the clearest terms possible.

Capital accumulation is another important contributor to economic growth. Thus, there is wisdom to the idea that a penny saved is a penny earned. More investment will generally lead to the kind of cautious growth that is more palatable to the public than disruptive technological change. However, there is such a thing as too much

Figure 7.1. Growth of US Regulation over Time

a. *US Code of Federal Regulations*, adjusted page count, 1949–2015

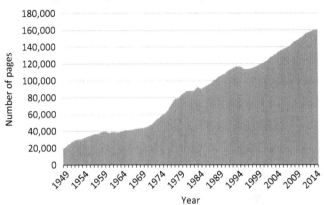

Note: Page count adjusted to exclude materials unrelated to private sector regulation and to account for stylistic changes in the code over time.

Source: Dawson and Seater 2013, data update to 2015 provided by the authors.

b. Regulatory restrictions in the *US Code of Federal Regulations*, 1975–2014

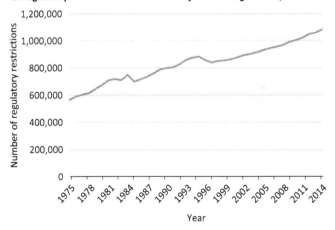

Source: Al-Ubaydli and McLaughlin 2015.

of a good thing. If the optimal level of capital per worker is exceeded, such as when the elasticity of substitution between capital and labor rises high enough, there may be reasons to limit capital accumulation. Furthermore, levels of consumption ultimately determine standards of living, so encouraging consumption can also make sense.

Human capital accumulation clearly matters, but job skills can come in many forms—from formal training to on-the-job experience. Obtaining both forms of skills requires tradeoffs. Competition policy is also important, and regulations that stifle competition by preventing new firms from entering an industry, setting maximum or minimum pricing, restricting quantities, or granting arbitrary monopoly privileges to firms or industries will stifle the learning-by-doing process, which is important to economic progress.

Trade also encourages growth by expanding the size of markets, allowing greater specialization, and transferring knowledge from one part of the globe to another. Intellectual property protections are also desirable, within reason. New technologies and global trade will not benefit everyone equally, however. There are important distributional consequences to consider. Over time, it may be become easier to substitute people with machines, and businesses will be attracted to the areas where labor is cheapest. At the very least, regulators should seek not to exacerbate inequalities that arise from these forces. They should not give an unfair advantage to capital over labor, and they should not create incentives whereby the best way to get ahead is through political connections and rent-seeking as opposed to serving customers.

Even if any single regulation is unlikely to produce growth rate effects, regulations should nurture and not stifle the factors known to be important for growth. These factors include productivity, investment, competition, human capital, institutions, and all the various forms of technological innovation.

After 60 years of modern economic growth theory, our ability to predict the growth implications of public policies may be better than many people realize. Yet given the vast uncertainties confronting regulators, a strong sense of humility is required. Critical puzzles in growth theory remain to be fully explained, and it is probably easier for regulators to slow economic growth than it is for them to accelerate it. Perhaps the framework presented here will help bridge theory and practice by providing a theoretical foundation for regulators. Such a foundation could move economics closer to solving the remaining puzzles while improving the design and implementation of the regulations that govern our lives.

ACKNOWLEDGMENTS

I would like to thank Tyler Cowen, Jerry Ellig, Garett Jones, Tracy Miller, and two anonymous peer reviewers for their helpful comments on this book. Any remaining mistakes are mine alone. I would also like to thank my wife, Anna, for enduring the long hours I worked in order to complete this project. Without her love and support, this book would not have been possible.

RECOMMENDED RESOURCES

Below is a list of resources for professors, students, policymakers, and others who wish to advance their understanding of regulation and economic growth beyond the general survey provided in this book.

ECONOMIC GROWTH MODELS

A useful survey of the models of economic growth is

Jones, Charles I. 2001. *Introduction to Economic Growth*, 2nd ed. New York: W. W. Norton.

For a more sophisticated review of the growth models, see

Barro, Robert J., and Xavier Sala-i-Martin. 2004. *Economic Growth*, 2nd ed. Cambridge, MA: MIT Press.

THE SOLOW MODEL

There are some useful online videos for those just getting introduced to the Solow Model. For example, see

Cowen, Tyler, and Alex Tarrabok. 2012. "The Solow Model 1—Introduction." Development Economics. Marginal Revolution University video, http://www.mruniversity.com/courses/development-economics/solow-model-1-%E2%80%93-introduction.

Berkeley professor Brad DeLong has a very handy Excel-based version of the Solow model, available at

DeLong, J. Bradford. 2006. "Solow Growth Model Scenario Generator Spreadsheet." http://delong.typepad.com/print/20060829_Solow_growth.xls

And, of course, there is the paper that started it all:

Solow, Robert M. 1956. "A Contribution to the Theory of Economic Growth." *Quarterly Journal of Economics* 70 (1): 65–94.

REGULATION

For an overview of the federal regulatory process in the United States, as well as a summary of the main theories used to explain regulation, see

Dudley, Susan E., and Jerry Brito. 2012. *Regulation: A Primer*, 2nd ed. Arlington, VA: Mercatus Center at George Mason University; Washington, DC: The George Washington University Regulatory Studies Center.

For recent estimates of the total cost of US federal regulation, see

Dawson, John W., and John J. Seater. 2013. "Federal Regulation and Aggregate Economic Growth." *Journal of Economic Growth* 18 (2): 137–77.

Coffey, Bentley, Patrick A. McLaughlin, and Pietro Peretto. 2016. "The Cumulative Cost of Regulations." Mercatus Working Paper. Arlington, VA: Mercatus Center at George Mason University.

Those looking for new ways of quantifying regulation in the United States should see

Al-Ubaydli, Omar, and Patrick A. McLaughlin. 2014. "RegData: A Numerical Database on Industry-Specific Regulations for All United States Industries and Federal Regulations, 1997–2012." Regulation and Governance, doi:10.1111/rego.12107.

Visit www.RegData.org and www.QuantGov.org to download data on regulatory restrictions in the United States.

DISCUSSION QUESTIONS

The following questions are designed for use in a classroom setting, to stimulate discussion or as a basis for homework assignments or exam exercises. The questions should also prove helpful for identifying original research topics related to the consequences of regulation for economic growth and living standards.

CHAPTER 1. INTRODUCTION

1. What is economic growth and why should anyone be concerned about it? Should other factors, such as factors that are not included in a measure like GDP, hold more weight with economists and policymakers?
2. What are regulations? How are legal and nonlegal regulations different from one another? How are they similar?

CHAPTER 2. THE FUNDAMENTALS OF ECONOMIC GROWTH

1. Aside from investing, name an example from everyday life where the power of compounding is present. What are the practical implications of an increase or a decrease in the growth rate or interest rate in your example?
2. How do the levels of income per person in table 2.2 correspond with what you think about living standards in different countries? Do they seem about right? In what ways do these numbers seem inaccurate? Are you surprised by which countries' economies grew relatively quickly or slowly during the period analyzed? Why or why not?
3. What are the two different types of economic growth? Why might one type of economic growth increase while the other decreases?
4. If a country's GDP is growing at 3 percent per year, how long will it take for national income to double? What about when the growth rate is 4 percent? Now consider that accompanying this 4 percent growth in GDP is population growth of 2 percent per year. How fast will GDP per capita double under these conditions? What if the population growth rate is 3 percent?

5. Which aspects of the Solow model are the most realistic in their portrayal of aspects of the real world? Which aspects of the model are the most unrealistic? Do the unrealistic aspects of the model limit the practical use of the model? Why or why not?

6. What is an economy's balanced growth path? How does it relate to an economy's steady state? What role does capital play with respect to these two concepts?

CHAPTER 3. CLASSIFICATION OF GROWTH EFFECTS

1. Explain (in words) the difference between a growth rate effect, a level effect, and a transitory growth effect.

2. University of California at Berkeley economist Bradford DeLong has created a useful Excel version of the Solow model. Download the Excel file (DeLong 2006, http://delong.typepad.com/print /20060829Solowgrowth.xls) and use it to produce graphs showing a negative growth rate effect, a positive level effect, and a negative transitory growth effect. Hint: This last graph may require some manipulations to the spreadsheet.

3. Looking at the DeLong Solow model spreadsheet, what role does the efficiency of labor play in the model? How does this relate to the concepts discussed in chapter 3 of this book? How does the efficiency of labor relate to the wages of workers?

4. What are the two different types of level effect? How are they similar and how do they differ?

5. What are the intragenerational and intergenerational distributional implications of the different types of growth effects? How might these differences in who receives the benefits of policy and who bears the costs affect which policies get adopted?

6. Name some potential future general purpose technologies that are not listed in table 3.1. What makes them likely to be GPTs?

7. How are the different types of growth effects related to one another? Why might these effects be difficult to distinguish in the real world?

8. What might be some reasons for the relatively persistent growth rate of income per person in the United States over the last century and a half?

9. The precautionary principle has been advanced as a way to protect the public from risky new technologies. What are the tradeoffs involved, from both an intragenerational and an intergenerational perspective, with letting the precautionary principle guide policy decisions?

CHAPTER 4. HOW REGULATIONS ENTER THE ECONOMIC SYSTEM

1. Why is the cumulative effect of all regulations together likely to have a bigger impact on GDP than the sum of the effects of all the same regulations viewed in isolation?

2. Provide an example of two real-world policies that interacted with one another, either beneficially or problematically, in a way that policymakers failed to anticipate.
3. Some highly specific products or technologies end up being vital inputs in complex production chains. Can you name a regulation that targeted a very specific production input of seemingly minor importance but that ended up having very broad consequences?
4. In an 1813 letter to Isaac McPherson, Thomas Jefferson wrote, "If nature has made any one thing less susceptible than all others of exclusive property, it is the actions of the thinking power called an idea, which an individual may exclusively possess as long as he keeps it to himself; but the moment it is divulged, it forces itself into the possession of every one, and the receiver cannot dispossess himself of it." Describe the relationship between ideas and property rights and the balancing act that is required when policymakers design patent protections.

CHAPTER 5. MODELS OF ECONOMIC GROWTH

1. What are the main differences between the models found in this chapter and the Solow model from chapter 2?
2. What are the different forms of innovation discussed in this chapter and how do they relate to human knowledge?
3. The Solow model suggests that the degree to which a country saves "only" produces a level effect, but other models suggest otherwise (e.g., the AK model). Which is right? What do the data say?
4. Consider the case where the government imposes a tax on all investments, such that a wedge is driven between the rate at which individuals lend to businesses and the rate of return that businesses must earn in order to justify borrowing at the market interest rate. How would this policy influence individual saving and consumption decisions? What effect would this policy have on economic growth in the different models?
5. Some knowledge is clearly excludable, while other knowledge is not. What are some examples of excludable and nonexcludable knowledge? How does "tacit knowledge," which cannot be easily written down or transmitted from one person to another, relate to excludability? Which models reviewed in this chapter best capture the concept of tacit knowledge?
6. What are the different types of catch-up growth? How does the phenomenon of diminishing returns lead to convergence in growth rates across countries, and even across firms?
7. How do externalities show up in growth models? What are some examples of growth models that incorporate externalities? Can you name any other externalities (positive or negative) occurring in the production process that could have spillover effects on growth?
8. Which models suggest that unintended consequences of human interaction contribute to economic growth? How does this phenomenon play out in the models? Which models describe growth as a more purposeful activity on the part of people?

9. What are some roles that the government can play to improve market allocations of resources? What information does a government need in order to respond effectively to the specific inefficiencies you identified?

10. What is the elasticity of substitution between capital and labor and how does it relate to inequality?

CHAPTER 6. THE ROLES OF INSTITUTIONS AND POPULATION

1. This book has discussed a range of possible outcomes that population growth can have on living standards. What do the different models of growth predict could occur owing to changes in population growth? Broadly speaking, is having more people on the planet good of bad for growth?

2. How might lessons from the growth models inform immigration policy? Does the type of immigration into a country matter for living standards? What about restrictions on the free movement of people within countries?

3. What variables do you think should be endogenized that have not been yet? How might economists go about explaining these variables in their models in the future?

4. What are institutions? What do you think of this term? Why might a catch-all term like "institutions" not be helpful when it comes to disentangling the different determinants of economic growth? How do institutions differ from policies enacted by governments?

5. Find a map and pick 15 countries that have area within 20 degrees of latitude (north or south) of the equator. Put together a table that lists the GDP per capita of each of these countries. Next create a table for 15 countries that are farther from the equator than 20 degrees of latitude. Create another table for countries that are landlocked (regardless of latitude). What lessons can you draw from this exercise?

CHAPTER 7. CONCLUSION

1. After reading this book, what do you think are the most important contributors to economic growth? What questions remain to be answered by growth economists in the future?

2. Which types of regulations are likely to most affect growth? Can you provide an example of a specific rule that may have produced a (positive or negative) growth *rate* effect? What is your evidence? Can you provide an example of a rule that may have produced a level effect or a transitory growth effect?

3. Go to www.regdata.org and download data on federal regulatory restrictions. Use the data to produce a list of the ten most-regulated industries for the most recent year data are available. Is there anything surprising about this list?

4. Is GDP a good measure of living standards? What are some of its limitations? What are its advantages? Is there another measure of living standards that is superior? If so, why?

NOTES

FOREWORD

1. Charles I. Jones, "The Facts of Economic Growth," version 2.0 (working paper, Stanford Graduate School of Business and National Bureau of Economic Research, December 18, 2015).

2. Bret Stephens, "Doomed to Stagnate?" *Wall Street Journal*, December 19, 2016.

CHAPTER 2. THE FUNDAMENTALS OF ECONOMIC GROWTH

1. See C. I. Jones (2000) and D. Romer (2011, 26) for specifics on how to obtain equation (2.7).

2. For example, see Barro and Sala-i-Martin (2004, 59).

CHAPTER 3. CLASSIFICATION OF GROWTH EFFECTS

1. Figure 3.1 as well as similar figures in this chapter were produced by modifying an impressive Excel version of the Solow model built by University of California at Berkeley economist Bradford DeLong (2006).

2. See Lipsey, Bekar, and Carlaw (1998) for an in-depth discussion of the definition of GPTs.

3. See Lipsey, Bekar, and Carlaw (2005, 379–84) for examples of such models.

4. See, for example, Conway et al. (2006); Égert (2016); Erlandsen and Lundsgaard (2007); Garicano, LeLarge, and Van Reenen (2013); and Nicoletti and Scarpetta (2003).

5. Note, however, that the level of the labor force has permanently increased.

6. The Car Allowance Rebate System, which came to be known as "cash for clunkers," was a 2009 federal program that provided incentives to consumers to turn in less fuel-efficient vehicles and purchase new, more fuel-efficient vehicles.

CHAPTER 5. MODELS OF ECONOMIC GROWTH

1. This expression is clearly an oversimplification, because some people who are not in the labor force will be doing things other than obtaining new skills.

2. For a description and an illustration of this point, see Weil (2013, 234).

CHAPTER 6. THE ROLES OF INSTITUTIONS AND POPULATION

1. For examples of this approach, see Hall and Jones (1999) and Knack and Keefer (1995).

2. See, for example, Montesquieu (1989 [1748]), who was an early observer of this fact.

REFERENCES

Abel, Andrew B., N. Gregory Mankiw, Lawrence H. Summers, and Richard J. Zeckhauser. 1989. "Assessing Dynamic Efficiency: Theory and Evidence." *Review of Economic Studies* 56 (1): 1-20.

Acemoglu, Daron, Simon Johnson, and James A. Robinson. 2001. "The Colonial Origins of Comparative Development: An Empirical Investigation." *American Economic Review* 91 (5): 1369-401.

———. 2005. "Institutions as a Fundamental Cause of Long-Run Growth." In *Handbook of Economic Growth*, vol. 1A, edited by Philippe Aghion and Steven N. Durlauf, 386-472. Amsterdam: Elsevier.

Aghion, Philippe, Yann Algan, Pierre Cahuc, and Andrei Shleifer. 2010. "Regulation and Distrust." *Quarterly Journal of Economics* 125 (3): 1015-49.

Aghion, Philippe, and Peter Howitt.1992. "A Model of Growth through Creative Destruction." *Econometrica* 60 (2): 323-51.

Alesina, Alberto, and Paola Giuliano. 2015. "Culture and Institutions." *Journal of Economic Literature* 53 (4): 898-944.

Al-Ubaydli, Omar, and Patrick A. McLaughlin. 2015. "RegData: A Numerical Database on Industry-Specific Regulations for All United States Industries and Federal Regulations, 1997-2012." *Regulation and Governance,* doi:10.1111/rego.12107.

Arrow, Kenneth J. 1962. "The Economic Implications of Learning by Doing." *Review of Economic Studies* 29 (3): 155-73.

Arrow, Kenneth J., Hollis B. Chenery, Bagicha S. Minhas, and Robert M. Solow. 1961. "Capital-Labor Substitution and Economic Efficiency." *Review of Economics and Statistics* 43 (3): 225-50.

Barro, Robert J. 1990. "Government Spending in a Simple Model of Endogenous Growth." *Journal of Political Economy* 98 (5): S103-26.

Barro, Robert J., and Xavier I. Sala-i-Martin. 2004. *Economic Growth*, 2nd ed. Cambridge, MA: MIT Press.

Bloom, David E., and Jeffrey D. Sachs. 1998. "Geography, Demography, and Economic Growth in Africa." *Brookings Papers on Economic Activity* 29 (2): 207-95.

Boldrin, Michele, and David K. Levine. 2008. *Against Intellectual Monopoly*. New York: Cambridge University Press.

Bresnahan, Timothy F., and Manuel Trajtenberg. 1995. "General Purpose Technologies 'Engines of Growth'?" *Journal of Econometrics* 65 (1): 83–108.

Caselli, Francesco. 2005. "Accounting for Cross-Country Income Differences." In *Handbook of Economic Growth*, vol. 1A, edited by Philippe Aghion and Steven N. Durlauf, 679–741. Amsterdam: North-Holland.

Cass, David. 1965. "Optimum Growth in an Aggregative Model of Capital Accumulation." *Review of Economic Studies* 32 (3): 233–40.

Chamberlin, Edward Hastings. 1933. *The Theory of Monopolistic Competition*. Cambridge, MA: Harvard University Press.

Chirinko, Robert S. 2008. "σ: The Long and Short of It." *Journal of Macroeconomics* 30 (2): 671–86.

Cobb, Charles W., and Paul H. Douglas. 1928. "A Theory of Production." *American Economic Review* 18 (1): 139–65.

Cochrane, John. 2015. "Smith Meet Jones." *The Grumpy Economist*, December 3. http://johnhcochrane.blogspot.ch/2015/12/smith-meet-jones.html.

Comin, Diego, William Easterly, and Erick Gong. 2010. "Was the Wealth of Nations Determined in 1000 BC?" *American Economic Journal: Macroeconomics* 2 (3): 65–97.

Conway, Paul, Donato de Rosa, Giuseppe Nicoletti, and Faye Steiner. 2006. "Regulation, Competition and Productivity Convergence" (OECD Economics Department Working Papers. Organisation for Economic Co-operation and Development, Paris).

Cowen, Tyler. 2011. *The Great Stagnation: How America Ate All the Low-Hanging Fruit of Modern History, Got Sick, and Will (Eventually) Feel Better*. New York: Dutton.

———. 2013. *Average Is Over: Powering America beyond the Age of the Great Stagnation*. New York: Dutton.

Dawson, John W., and John J. Seater. 2013. "Federal Regulation and Aggregate Economic Growth." *Journal of Economic Growth* 18 (2): 137–77.

DeLong, J. Bradford. 2006. "Brad DeLong's Solow Growth Model Scenario Generator Spreadsheet." http://delong.typepad.com/print/20060829_Solow_growth.xls.

Diamond, Jared. 1997. *Guns, Germs, and Steel: The Fates of Human Societies*. New York: Norton.

Dixit, Avinash K., and Joseph Stiglitz. 1977. "Monopolistic Competition and Optimum Product Diversity." *American Economic Review* 67 (3): 297–308.

Domar, Evsey D. 1946. "Capital Expansion, Rate of Growth, and Employment." *Econometrica* 14 (2): 137–47.

Dourado, Eli, and Alex Tabarrok. 2015. "Public Choice Perspectives on Intellectual Property." *Public Choice* 163 (1): 129–51.

Égert, Balázs. 2016. "Regulation, Institutions, and Productivity: New Macroeconomic Evidence from OECD Countries." *American Economic Review* 106 (5): 109–13.

Erlandsen, Espen, and Jens Lundsgaard. 2007. "How Regulatory Reforms in Sweden Have Boosted Productivity" (OECD Economics Department Working Paper, Organisation for Economic Co-operation and Development, Paris).

Feenstra, Robert C., Robert Inklaar, and Marcel Timmer. 2013. "The Next Generation of the Penn World Table" (NBER Working Paper No. 19255, National Bureau of Economic Research, Cambridge, MA).

———. 2015. "The Next Generation of the Penn World Table." *American Economic Review* 105 (10): 3150–82.

Frankel, Marvin. 1962. "The Production Function in Allocation and Growth: A Synthesis." *American Economic Review* 52 (5): 996–1022.

Galor, Oded, and Ömer Özak. 2014. "The Agricultural Origins of Time Preference" (NBER Working Paper No. 20438, National Bureau of Economic Research, Cambridge, MA).

Garicano, Luis, Claire LeLarge, and John Van Reenen. 2013. "Firm Size Distortions and the Productivity Distribution: Evidence from France" (NBER Working Paper No. 18841, National Bureau of Economic Research, Cambridge, MA).

Grossman, Gene M., and Elhanan Helpman. 1991. "Quality Ladders in the Theory of Growth." *Review of Economic Studies* 58 (1): 43–61.

Hall, Robert E., and Charles I. Jones. 1999. "Why Do Some Countries Produce So Much More Output per Worker than Others?" *Quarterly Journal of Economics* 114 (1): 83–116.

Harrod, Roy F. 1939. "An Essay in Dynamic Theory." *Economic Journal* 49 (193): 14–33.

Hayek, Friedrich A. 1984 [1968]. "Competition as a Discovery Procedure." In *The Essence of Hayek*, edited by Chiaki Nishiyama and Kurt R. Leube, 254–65. Stanford, CA: Hoover Institution Press.

Heller, Michael A. 1998. "The Tragedy of the Anticommons: Property in the Transition from Marx to Markets." *Harvard Law Review* 111 (3): 621–88.

Hsieh, Chang-Tai, Erik Hurst, Charles I. Jones, and Peter J. Klenow. 2013. "The Allocation of Talent and U.S. Economic Growth" (NBER Working Paper No. 18693, National Bureau of Economic Research, Cambridge, MA).

Inada, Ken-Ichi. 1963. "On a Two-Sector Model of Economic Growth: Comments and a Generalization." *Review of Economic Studies* 30 (2): 119–27.

Jones, Charles I. 1995. "Time Series Tests of Endogenous Growth Models." *Quarterly Journal of Economics* 110 (2): 495–525.

——. 1999. "Growth: With or Without Scale Effects?" *American Economic Review* 89 (2): 139–44.

——. 2000. "A Note on the Closed-Form Solution of the Solow Model." http://web.stanford.edu/~chadj/closedform.pdf.

——. 2001. *Introduction to Economic Growth*, 2nd ed. New York: Norton.

——. 2013. "Misallocation, Economic Growth, and Input-Output Economics." In *Advances in Economics and Econometrics*, Tenth World Congress, vol. II, *Applied Economics*, edited by Daron Acemoglu, Manuel Arellano, and Eddie Dekel. Cambridge: Cambridge University Press.

——. 2015. "The Facts of Economic Growth" (NBER Working Paper No. 21142, National Bureau of Economic Research, Cambridge, MA).

Jones, Charles I, and Paul M. Romer. 2010. "The New Kaldor Facts: Ideas, Institutions, Population, and Human Capital." *American Economic Journal: Macroeconomics* 2 (1): 224–45.

Jones, Garett. 2012. "Cognitive Skill and Technology Diffusion: An Empirical Test." *Economic Systems* 36 (3): 444–60.

——. 2015. *Hive Mind: How Your Nation's IQ Matters So Much More Than Your Own*. Stanford, CA: Stanford University Press.

Jovanovic, Boyan, and Peter L. Rousseau. 2005. "General Purpose Technologies." In *Handbook of Economic Growth*, vol. 1B, edited by Philippe Aghion and Steven N. Durlauf, 1181–224. New York: Elsevier.

Kaldor, Nicholas. 1961. "Capital Accumulation and Economic Growth." In *The Theory of Capital*, 177–222. New York: Macmillan.

Knack, Stephen, and Philip Keefer. 1995. "Institutions and Economic Performance: Cross-Country Tests Using Alternative Institutional Measures." *Economics and Politics* 7 (3): 207–27.

Koopmans, Tjalling C. 1965. "On the Concept of Optimal Economic Growth" (Discussion Paper No. 163, Cowles Foundation for Research in Economics at Yale University, New Haven, CT).

Kremer, Michael. 1993a. "The O-Ring Theory of Economic Development." *Quarterly Journal of Economics* 108 (3): 551–75.

——. 1993b. "Population Growth and Technological Change: One Million B.C. to 1990." *Quarterly Journal of Economics* 108 (3): 681–716.

Krugman, Paul. 1980. "Scale Economies, Product Differentiation, and the Pattern of Trade." *American Economic Review* 70 (5): 950–59.

Leontief, Wassily W. 1941. *The Structure of American Economy, 1919–1929*. Cambridge, MA: Harvard University Press.

Lipsey, Richard G., Cliff Bekar, and Kenneth Carlaw. 1998. "What Requires Explanation?" In *General Purpose Technologies and Economic Growth*, edited by Elhanan Helpman, 15–54. Cambridge, MA: MIT Press.

——. *Economic Transformations: General Purpose Technologies and Long Term Economic Growth*. New York: Oxford University Press.

Lucas, Robert E. Jr. 1988. "On the Mechanics of Economic Development." *Journal of Monetary Economics* 22 (1): 3–42.

Malthus, Thomas Robert. 1798. *An Essay on the Principle of Population*. London: J. Johnson, in St. Paul's Church-Yard.

Mandel, Michael J. 2004. *Rational Exuberance: Silencing the Enemies of Growth and Why the Future Is Better Than You Think*. New York: HarperCollins.

Mandel, Michael, and Diana G. Carew. 2013. "Regulatory Improvement Commission: A Politically-Viable Approach to U.S. Regulatory Reform" (Policy Memo, Progressive Policy Institute, Washington, DC).

Mankiw, N. Gregory, David Romer, and David N. Weil. 1992. "A Contribution to the Empirics of Economic Growth." *Quarterly Journal of Economics* 107 (2): 407–37.

Montesquieu, Charles de Secondat. 1989 [1748]. *The Spirit of the Laws*, translated and edited by Anne M. Cohler, Basia Carolyn Miller, and Harold Samuel Stone. New York: Cambridge University Press.

Nicoletti, Giuseppe, and Stefano Scarpetta. 2003. "Regulation, Productivity, and Growth: OECD Evidence" (Policy Research Working Paper WPS2944, World Bank, Washington, DC).

North, Douglass C. 1991. "Institutions." *Journal of Economic Perspectives* 5 (1): 97–112.

OECD (Organisation for Economic Co-operation and Development). 2003. *The Sources of Economic Growth in OECD Countries*. Paris: OECD.

Piketty, Thomas. 2014. *Capital in the Twenty-First Century*. Cambridge, MA: Harvard University Press.

Ramsey, Frank P. 1928. "A Mathematical Theory of Saving." *Economic Journal* 38 (152): 543–59.

Rebelo, Sergio. 1991. "Long-Run Policy Analysis and Long-Run Growth." *Journal of Political Economy* 99 (3): 500–521.

Rodrik, Dani, Arvind Subramanian, and Francesco Trebbi. 2004. "Institutions Rule: The Primacy of Institutions over Geography and Integration in Economic Development." *Journal of Economic Growth* 9 (2): 131–65.

Rognlie, Matthew. 2015. "Deciphering the Fall and Rise in the Net Capital Share" (Brookings Paper on Economic Activity, Brookings Institution, Washington, DC).

Romer, David. 2011. *Advanced Macroeconomics*, 4th ed. New York: McGraw-Hill.

Romer, Paul M. 1986. "Increasing Returns and Long-Run Growth." *Journal of Political Economy* 94 (5): 1002–37.

———. 1990. "Endogenous Technological Change." *Journal of Political Economy* 98 (5): S71–102.

Sachs, Jeffrey D. 2003. "Institutions Don't Rule: Direct Effects of Geography on per Capita Income" (NBER Working Paper No. 9490, National Bureau of Economic Research, Cambridge, MA).

Schumpeter, Joseph. 1942. *Capitalism, Socialism and Democracy*. New York: Harper & Brothers.

Smith, James P. 1999. "Healthy Bodies and Thick Wallets: The Dual Relation between Health and Economic Status." *Journal of Economic Perspectives* 13 (2): 145–66.

Solow, Robert M. 1956. "A Contribution to the Theory of Economic Growth." *Quarterly Journal of Economics* 70 (1): 65–94.

Spolaore, Enrico, and Romain Wacziarg. 2013. "How Deep Are the Roots of Economic Development?" *Journal of Economic Literature* 51 (2): 325–69.

Swan, Trevor W. 1956. "Economic Growth and Capital Accumulation." *Economic Record* 32 (2): 334–61.

Thierer, Adam. 2016. *Permissionless Innovation: The Continuing Case for Comprehensive Technological Freedom*, revised and expanded edition. Arlington, VA: Mercatus Center at George Mason University.

Uzawa, Hirofumi. 1964. "Optimal Growth in a Two-Sector Model of Capital Accumulation." *Review of Economic Studies* 31 (1): 1–24.

Weber, Max. 1930 [1904]. *The Protestant Ethic and the Spirit of Capitalism*. London and New York: Routledge.

Weil, David N. 2013. *Economic Growth*, 3rd ed. London: Routledge.

Yellen, Janet. 1984. "Efficiency Wage Models of Unemployment." *American Economic Review* 74 (2): 200–205.

Zak, Paul J., and Stephen Knack. 2001. "Trust and Growth." *Economic Journal* 111 (470): 295–321.

ABOUT THE AUTHOR

James Broughel is a research fellow for the State and Local Policy Project at the Mercatus Center at George Mason University and an adjunct professor of law at the Antonin Scalia Law School. He specializes in the economic analysis of regulations, state and federal regulatory procedures, and economic growth.

Broughel has authored numerous policy briefs and reports on regulatory issues. His work has appeared in outlets such as *U.S. News & World Report*, *Real Clear Policy*, *The Hill*, *Yahoo Finance*, the *Louisville Courier-Journal*, the *Washington Times*, and the *Washington Examiner*. He has published in scholarly journals, including the *Harvard Journal of Law & Public Policy: Federalist Edition* and the *European Journal of Risk Regulation*.

Broughel received his PhD in economics from George Mason University in 2017 and his BA and MA in economics from Hunter College of the City University of New York, from which he graduated summa cum laude.

Made in the USA
Middletown, DE
18 May 2017